Praise for *Ho[w]*

Cindy's book, *How Coul[d ...]*
that when we surround our lives with so much chaos—we
run the risk of missing out on all God has for us.

—Michael W. Smith, Grammy and Dove Award–winning
singer/songwriter, American Music Award recipient

An artist is defined as "one who practices any of the fine or
performing arts, as painting or music." Cindy Morgan is an
artist in the real sense of the word: She paints with beautiful
words and sings with amazing colors, she inspires me to want
to reach deeper and climb higher, and somehow she points
me to Christ with her fine art.

—Tom Douglas, songwriter, CMA Song of the Year winner
("The House That Built Me"), Grammy Award winner

How Could I Ask for More is twenty years overdue. At least,
that's how long we've been waiting for Cindy to write this
book. Since we have known her, Cindy has told stories of
her family, her friendships, and now Sigmund and her
girls, in ways that draw us in with humor and warmth, and
always lead us to a place of gratitude. She paints a picture
with her words and stories that expresses both our humanity
and God's undeniable goodness to us in the midst of that
humanity. We know this book will do the same for you as she
has for us for these past twenty years: lead you, with humor
and great humility, to a place of deep, deep gratitude.

—Sissy Goff & Melissa Trevathan, authors of six books including
Intentional Parenting, curriculum (*Raising Boys and Girls*),
counselors at Daystar Counseling Ministries

Over the past fifteen years, I have learned that the heart of Cindy Morgan is as tender, passionate, and beautiful as the songs that pour forth from it. Readers will now be able to know and experience more of that incredible heart, as it is revealed in the pages of *How Could I Ask for More*. The simplicity and authenticity of her stories, and the depth of the lessons they teach, offer a rich opportunity for reflection.

—Ginny Owens, singer/songwriter,
professor of songwriting at Belmont University

In *How Could I Ask for More* Cindy Morgan weaves mystical stories of love, loss, and redemption from her childhood in rural Tennessee to her rise as one of Christian music's most important and celebrated voices. Her wit and colorful observations makes this page-turner a joyful ride for the entire family.

—David Perozzi, ABC News,
senior producer for Barbara Walters

There really is something special about Cindy Morgan; her works of art are comfortable and captivating. Cindy has an endless quality of intrigue, which presents itself through many different forms—songwriting, singing, writing, worship. She is a true artist and I admire her.

—Jaci Velasquez, singer, actress, television host,
Dove Award winner and Grammy nomineee

In *How Could I Ask for More* Cindy shows how the good things in life are really the God things. Mixing scripture with stories of her life and experiences, Cindy helps sharpen the reader's focus on the gifts of God that are profound in their simplicity.

—Paige Clayton Greene, director of adult events (including all Beth Moore conferences), LifeWay Christian Resources

You have heard the adage "When the rubber meets the road." Now get ready to experience it. Cindy has the ability and insight to make us look introspectively, dig deeper, and focus on the real reason why we are on this earth. Her optimism rises from the ashes of pessimism and brings fresh inspiration to life. Cindy will challenge, inspire, and touch you. She will help you see that change must begin internally before it can become external. Thank you, Cindy, for opening your heart and sharing your desires, failures, and successes.

—Pastor Gerald McGinnis (Cindy's pastor of twenty years), lead pastor of Parkwest Church in Knoxville Tennessee, and chaplain to the FBI

CINDY MORGAN

how could I ask for more

STORIES *of*
BLESSINGS, BATTLES, & BEAUTY

WORTHY®
Inspired

Copyright © 2015 by Cindy Morgan

ISBN 978-1-61795-655-3

Published by Worthy Inspired, an imprint of Worthy Publishing Group, a division of
Worthy Media, Inc., One Franklin Park, 6100 Tower Circle, Suite 210, Franklin, TN
37067.

Library of Congress Control Number: 2015942793

"How You Live (Turn Up the Music)," words and music by Cindy Morgan, © Lola Max
Music (ASCAP), Word Music (ASCAP).

"Breaking Heart," music by Cindy Morgan, words by Cindy Morgan and Chris Donohue,
© Checkpointchicky Music (BMI) administered by Music Services, Inc., and Canto68
Music (SEASAC), administered by PJ Heimermann @ Fun Attic Music.

Scripture quotations marked ESV are from THE ENGLISH STANDARD VERSION. ©
2001 by Crossway Bibles, a division of Good News Publishers.

Scripture quotations marked KJV are from the King James Version.

Scripture quotations marked NIV are from the Holy Bible, New International Version®,
NIV®. Copyright © 1973, 1978, 1984, 2011 by Biblica, Inc.™ Used by permission of
Zondervan. All rights reserved worldwide. www.zondervan.com

Scripture quotations marked NKJV are from THE NEW KING JAMES VERSION. ©
1982 by Thomas Nelson, Inc. Used by permission. All rights reserved.

All rights reserved. No part of this publication may be reproduced, stored in a
retrieval system, or transmitted in any form or by any means—electronic, mechanical,
photocopy, recording, scanning, or other—except for brief quotations in critical reviews
or articles, without the prior written permission of the publisher.

Cover Design by Greg Jackson/ThinkPen Designs
For photo credits, see pages 195–202

Printed in the United States of America

1 2 3 4 5—LBM—19 18 17 16 15

IN MEMORY OF COVA MORGAN.
YOUR LIFE STILL SPEAKS TODAY.

Contents

Foreword

I remember the first time I heard Cindy Morgan sing live. The old barn cupped by wistful hills on a Tennessee farm was the perfect setting for her soaring vocals and earthy nature. She was performing at a hymn-sing to help raise money for a local ministry that pours into the lives of children with the love of Jesus. My first impression of Cindy, beyond her exquisite songwriting and transcendent vocals, was that she was generous—generous with her talents, her time, and her very being. That summer's eve, Cindy took those hymns and sang them to the moon and back, and she lit a passion in my heart to take the melodies and musings I'd been given and offer them for the glory of God and for the blessing of others.

Since that day I've been the happy recipient of Cindy's poetic thoughts set to melodies that slip inside your head and make their home there. Some of them I've been singing since I was in college, her lyrics helping shape my faith and giving voice to prayers and praises I couldn't quite find my own words for. And then there was the day, many years later, she showed up at my house to co-write a song with me, and I was so nervous I couldn't think of one decent line. Out of Cindy tumbled lyrics and chord voicings and harmonies so effortlessly, but it was her kindness, the time she took with me, the encouraging words that have stayed with me.

You can imagine how thrilled I was to find that Cindy would be taking her mind and creativity to pen and paper, what you're holding in your hands. I have always been one to enjoy peeking into the lives of those whose artistry I so respect, wondering what painful turns and lonely twists brought them to write and sing what they do. More than anything, beholding the ways God gripped their wrists and held their hearts through the joys and trials of life. Cindy not only gives us these glimpses, but she challenges us along the way. Pushing us toward more of Christ, the way she's been mercifully prodded.

I'm already grateful for the journey you'll be taking through these pages. If for no other reason than that Cindy has a way of taking the common and pulling back its curtain, reminding us that what we see every day, the textures we touch, the fragrances we smell, our ransom that's been dearly paid, and inspires us to ask the question: indeed, how could we ask for more?

Kelly Minter

Singer/songwriter, speaker, and author of
No Other Gods: Confronting Our Modern Day Idols,
Ruth: Loss, Love & Legacy, and *Nehemiah: A Heart That Can Break*

How Could I Ask for More

Everyone has a dream. My mother dreamed of being a missionary. My brother dreamed of being an artist but ended up being a trucker. My friend Val Arnold dreamed of being a homeschool mom and driving a minivan. Your dream might be something very different: NASCAR driver, Broadway performer, or something as unlikely as a funeral home director.

It is the thing that beckons to us from within, the desire and the gifting that God places inside each of us. The role we are summoned to play that brings balance and rightness to the world.

For me, like my father before me, that dream was to be a writer—to write songs and to sing them. But the dream we set out to achieve can lead us down roads we never expected, require sacrifices, and carry heartaches we don't think we can bear. Is it worth it to live the life we feel called to—even if there will be as many battles as there are blessings? As much brash as there is beauty? I have caught a glimpse of what lies on the other side of the battleground. The real promised land. I have seen the sparkling gold at the end of the rainbow.

What is it?

I'll get to that.

The *why* that fuels the dream is something that has kept me up many nights. Our need to reach the next big thing, the next goal, the next mountain to conquer will always leave us wandering around in the forest unable to see the beautiful tree growing by the water, or in the clearing, or . . . Our eyes cannot behold true beauty within the dream itself. It might just look like a common poplar at first, before we see the shimmering golden leaves of fall. Where is the dream taking us? What is the destination point of the dream?

Before we find our way to this answer, we live with the feeling that there must be more. Somehow we have been led to believe that *more* is the key to happiness. And to the dream.

More money. More success. More friends. More kids. More love. More sex. More alcohol. More. More. More.

I was around nineteen when my mother loaned me her red VW Beetle to make the drive from East Tennessee to Nashville to meet with John Mays from Word Records. John had invited me to lunch after listening to a copy of my demo that he'd received from my friend Kirk Talley. As we ate Mexican food, I stared across the table wondering how in the world God had brought a girl from a small log cabin, in a snake-infested holler in East Tennessee (aptly nicknamed Snake Holler) to this moment. John eventually signed me to a record deal—changing the course of my life forever.

When that moment came for me to follow the path that might lead to my dream, I packed up my clothes and my Casio keyboard and moved to Nashville. I worked in retail and as a waitress while I made my first record, *Real Life*. I would change out of my waitress uniform at a Wendy's bathroom down the street from Word before I stopped by to see John. Some days, I would have a new song to play for him. Other days, we would talk about books, life, and perspective. To this day, I will never really be able to express what John's mentorship meant to me then and still means to me today. He taught me about being human, about caring for others, about looking past the surface to the deeper and beautiful things of life.

I started on the long journey of playing song after song for both John and producer Mark Hammond. I was in what a record company calls a development deal, which means they take you for a test-drive, let you write (and record) a few songs, and see if they think you have what it takes. I recall these as golden days—but also a very stressful period of life. The pressure to do well on the test was enormous. Almost doesn't cut it and I am a pleaser by nature—a scenario made for sleepless nights and ulcers. Oh, but for the grace of God.

John had laid down a challenge for me to write a song that would be kind of a signature song. Something that would express who I was at heart.

I wrote song after song, late at night, keeping my roommate, Michelle, up all hours of the night (sorry, Michelle) trying to get at the song they were hoping for. I would play Mark and John song after song but again and again they would smile and say, "It's good, but dig a little deeper, bleed a little more."

I was bleeding all right. But not enough.

One day, after I had played them yet another rejected new song, I left the meeting crushed. After throwing a few clothes in a bag and jumping in the red VW that had become mine (thanks, Mom), I drove east on I-40 to see my family and some close friends. I needed to get away from the feeling of failure. The feeling of not measuring up and the fear of what price might have to be paid to get the results John and Mark were looking for.

I drove along as the sun was setting. The moon started to come into focus in the Tennessee sky. It dawned on me that I was on the cusp of having everything I had ever dreamed of, but *I wasn't cutting it*. I was about to blow my only good chance at my dream. I considered what I might do if I failed. What about my life was still valuable? If I lost my record deal and had to move back to East Tennessee, could I still live out a good life? What was most important to me in life? All these questions ran through my nineteen-year-old brain as I drove.

The moon shone brightly through my window while my mind wandered to memories of growing up as a child—the good moments of life, the things that breathed peace and comfort into the chaos. I had a number 2 pencil and a spiral notebook on the empty passenger seat. With one hand on the steering wheel, I wrote down lyrics with the other (eyes on the road!). The words ran down the page in a gradual descent, barely legible.

There's nothing like the warmth of a summer afternoon, waking to the sunlight and being cradled by the moon . . .

As the miles went by, the words poured out onto the page like the moonlight pouring in through my windows. The melody was suddenly in my head. To recall it today, it almost seems like a dream. To this day, I believe God simply gave that song to me. By the time I reached my destination, the song was just shy of a last verse from being written. I called it "How Could I Ask for More."

When I had my next meeting with John and Mark, I took a deep breath and played them the song from my moonlit drive. As I played the last note, I looked up and saw tears in John's eyes. It was a moment I will never forget.

I have sung this song hundreds of times. At weddings, funerals, small churches, coliseums, and graduations. I have loved hearing what the song has meant to others. I thank God that John and Mark pushed me. They didn't let me settle for almost.

I have always believed that in order to connect you have to be willing to be honest. You have to be brave and put the truth on the page.

That is what I have attempted to do in these chapters ahead. I am writing to you as if I know you, and you know me. As if we might meet for coffee next week and talk about the kids or a doctor's visit you're concerned about or about a ghost you can't quite shake.

Writers call that *writing with the door closed*—as opposed to *writing with the door open*, in which you shy away from writing things that are too personal, too telling. I thought I would just tell how it really was and how it really is and let my editor tell me when I've gone too far. (Thanks, Jamie.)

Why?

Because I want to remind myself of the other thing I learned in the process of writing this song that has meant so much to me. I gained a pair of new eyes that day—eyes to see what still mattered in life. You need those eyes when things aren't going your way and your big dream kind of looks a bit more like a nightmare. There is always joy to be found and a peace that abides within us. Sometimes the most extraordinary things are just the ordinary things that we finally see the true worth of. Like a rising moon, a child's smile, or your mother's voice.

I don't want to lose that way of seeing. And I want to remind myself of the things in life that matter. Of what I have learned from loss and heartache and the beauty that often follows after loss.

Sometimes we have to burn off the superficial to get down to the things in life that really matter. God will never ask you or me to sacrifice our family, our morals, or those we love for a dream. When we hold tight to those fragile moments that create who we are, when we recognize the difference between what is sacred and what is superficial—that is when the clear vision for a worthy dream starts to come into focus.

I want to tell you what my own journey has taught me. Stories of how God has shown Himself to me. Moments when I have walked away from God and what the road looked like walking back. I want to share my fears and my longings and those rare moments when you catch a glimpse of the truth.

There is a prayer I pray almost every day. Sometimes while I am rushing out the door, late for a writing appointment, sometimes in the middle of the night when I cannot sleep for the worries that find me in the dark. I pray,

Oh, Lord, give me eyes to see, ears to hear, and a heart to understand.

Eyes to see what matters and to look away from the things that cause me to stumble. To fear.

Ears to hear the words that bring life. To speak words that build up and silence the words that tear down.

A heart to understand the immeasurable joy we have been given in life. The treasure of living and loving and weeping and falling down and getting back up. That each moment in life, when surrendered to You, God, can be a treasure. Even the difficult ones.

There is an old saying: Yesterday is history, tomorrow is a mystery, today is a gift of God, which is why we call it the present. How could I ask for more?

Ringing Bells

As a child, I remember just over the fence of our backyard was a Baptist church with a tall, white steeple and a bell that rang out every Sunday morning at nine for Sunday school and ten for worship.

This was at a time when my family was in recovery from the loss of my brother Samuel, who had died a year and a half before from an aggressive blood cancer. He'd been one week shy of his fifth birthday. My siblings were older, teenagers at the time. I was around five and a half.

My dad was a Volkswagen mechanic and worked every day but Sunday trying to pay off the enormous mound of hospital bills left over from Samuel's treatments and the long stay in the hospital before his passing.

I cannot imagine anything more depressing than working six days a week, twelve hours a day to pay off a debt for something that ultimately resulted in the loss of what was so precious to him—his youngest son.

At this time in my family, it seemed we were each going our own way, trying to grab on to something solid. My mother was involved in a charismatic church that fancied praying in Hebrew. They met in an old house and were given to prophetic utterances more than biblical teaching. I remember attending one of their meetings, sitting in a corner on the hardwood floor. The preacher (who looked very much like a mattress salesman) wore a brown polyester suit and had a greasy comb-over. To "bless" his congregation, he placed each of them (all of his followers were women . . . ahh-hem), one at a time, in a kitchen chair while he pronounced prophetic utterances, flailed his arms, and danced, John Travolta-ish, around the chair. That was my last visit to my mom's church.

My sister Sam drove herself to a church she'd found that had a thriving youth group. When the weather was warm she played hooky and went to the lake with friends. My brother Mike had decided to join the army at the end of his junior year in high school.

So most Sunday mornings it was just me and my dad. Sunday was his only day to rest, and though he was a man of devout faith, he had been burned by a few less-than-trustworthy preachers over the years—most recently by the "holy" men who attempted to convince both him and my mother that if they truly believed, Samuel would be healed. At the end of Samuel's life, my father was left with a gaping hole and the words of these charlatans ringing in his ears. This tended to give him a completely different feeling when he heard the ringing of the church bell each Sunday morning. He sat in his green recliner drinking strong coffee, watching Jimmy Swaggart on TV, trying to forget.

But when that bell rang over the fence, it called to me.

It called for reasons I could not understand or explain but it pulled me like a magnet, like a string tethered to me, connected to someone or something on the other end that I could not see . . . 'til one Sunday, I woke up and asked my father if it would be okay if I attended the church over the fence by myself.

A sad smile ran across his face before he said he thought that would be fine; he knew the pastor and a few of their members were customers of his. A few minutes before the nine o'clock bell rang, my dad walked me to the edge of the yard and waved as I climbed the steep steps of the First Baptist Church of Harrogate.

I remember how grand the ladies looked in their summer bonnets and large strands of pearls clasped around their necks. It was an elegant church where elderly men smelled of Old Spice and the Sunday school teachers gave you a lollipop just for showing up.

There was a boy from my class at school who attended there; it was nice to see a familiar face, but even still, this was a time in my life when I felt alone. I was living inside myself, as my whole family seemed to be doing as we struggled to cope with our grief. Trying to grasp something that would hold. Waiting for a seed to be planted in fertile ground.

So Sunday after Sunday I crossed the fence as the bell rang and sat by myself in the back pew. Pressing my scuffed Mary Janes into the plush red carpet as I sat and listened to Pastor Shown. One day, toward the end of the service, he raised a question.

Do you know Jesus?

Do you hear Him calling you?
Do you want Him to come into your heart?

These were familiar words to me, living with a devout/ fanatical mother who was constantly worried her children would grow up to be godless heathens. She must have asked each of us those same questions a few dozen times. But somehow, that day, with the sun shining in through the stained-glass windows, this question rang in my ears louder than those church bells ever had.

Suddenly I wondered, *Is He talking to me?* I had this feeling inside, as if that string that had been pulling me to church was suddenly tugging a little more insistently. What was at the other end?

The altar.

Those first few steps down the aisle were terrifying. So many people staring at the shy girl in a secondhand dress with no ribbons in her barely brushed hair . . . with a longing to know. *Who is Jesus?* There was a longing inside, you see, to understand life and loss and pain and whether there was any meaning to it all.

As I knelt there at the altar of that Baptist church, a light came on inside me. I suddenly felt something I didn't even realize I had lost.

Hope.

Up until then my hope had been rooted in my parents' hope, but the pain of their loss had robbed them of it, leaving me to draw living water out of a nearly empty well.

I didn't realize that what my heart was longing for every time I heard the church bell ring in my backyard, was a sense of hope. Of purpose. Life without it can seem as futile as paying off a hospital debt for a dead son.

My father, I would later understand, found meaning in his long hours of working overtime to pay off the medical bills while supporting his family. He saw each of us as a gift, more precious now, he understood, than before the loss of his youngest son. He paid every single penny of the debt as a last way to honor Samuel. He never once complained about those bills. He knew why he was doing it.

A few Sundays after my walk down the aisle, I stood shivering in the baptistry wearing a white cotton gown with my mother, father, sister, and the rest of the church staring up at me. As Pastor Shown plunged me under the water I came up breathless but filled with a certainty that there was something more to my life than I could have known. To serve the one who had created me. The one who knew every pain I had ever felt, who knew each turn my life would take. Through the dark cloud hanging over our lives, a shaft of sunlight broke through.

Life had purpose. I knew Jesus and He knew me. And I wondered if in heaven, maybe there was an angel, a boy with my same eyes, who was looking on as the church bells rang. As if they were ringing just for me.

What Is Your Why?

IT SOUNDS A LITTLE LIKE a tongue twister or some kind of trick question on the Enneagram personality test.

I have asked myself this question many times. Most people have, I would guess.

You wake up one morning and realize you are in a job you hate, a marriage that is difficult on the best of days, and you look at the years passing by like the treadmill is turned up full-blast. And you ask yourself, *Why am I doing this? What am I doing with my life?*

Your *why* is your bigger purpose. Your calling. The thing that gets you out of bed when you don't think you can.

The demands of life are fierce, and it is easy to get caught on that treadmill. You might wait years before you ask the question, *Why?* The whys drive everything, whether we realize it or not.

In my life as a songwriter, I have been mentoring young (female) singer/songwriters who are just starting, trying to find their voice and their path as artists.

I ask them the why question: *Right now, in the fresh dirt of your new life, ask yourself what your motivation is. Why do you want to write songs? What do you hope comes out of your artistry?* I ask this because—I know this now—one day in the not-so-distant future, they will find themselves overwhelmed and fatigued and frustrated and they will want to give up; and at that point, there is only one thing that will keep them from throwing in the towel and walking away. The why.

On the surface it might seem that there could be no greater or more motivating why than success, which can look like financial security, peer respect, or even worldwide fame.

I read a novel a few years ago that changed my perspective about life, so it seems appropriate to bring it up. Jonas Crow's life starts out as normal as most, but when Jonas is very young both his parents die. For a few happy years he lives with an elderly aunt and uncle, but when they, too, pass away he is taken to live in an orphanage, where his entire identity is reduced to his first initial J. It is a cold and unloving place. When he is old enough to leave the orphanage he eventually makes his way to a small town along a river in Kentucky and becomes the town's only barber and, eventually, a gravedigger and church custodian. This character's why was to find what he had been robbed of: family, community, friends, a name. To belong. But also to be a friend. To be family to others. To offer community to those who felt like outsiders. To give what he himself longed for.

I have a friend whose father was a mortician for the only funeral home in their small town back around where I'm from in East Tennessee. While this man was the mortician, he was present for the death of every person in town. Mothers dying in childbirth, a child drowning, a young teenager dying in a car accident. Can you imagine? He was there to carry them out of their houses if they died at home, hold the weeping loved ones consumed by grief, embalm the deceased, help the family pick out the casket, the hymns for the service . . . and dig the grave and cover it over with earth at the end. Sometimes he paid for the funeral himself, for those who were too poor to afford one. As I sat there listening to his story I was overwhelmed by the impact his career choice had made on so many. The enormous power of knowing your why has never seemed so poignant as it was in this man's life. To care for others. To find community. To be a friend to someone. To offer words of comfort and support in the darkest hour. To help the less fortunate. Like the words of Isaiah: *The Spirit of the LORD is upon me, because the LORD has anointed me to preach good tidings to the poor . . . to heal the brokenhearted . . . to comfort all who mourn . . . to give them beauty for ashes* (see Isaiah 61:1–3).

On the other end of the spectrum you often see big Hollywood stars or rock stars who attach themselves to a cause. These people, you will notice, tend to have staying power, and I am convinced it is because they know what their why is.

They don't do it so they can have a few more million dollars in their bank account or a bigger star on the Walk of Fame. They have broken through the superficial facade of stardom and found something deeper and more meaningful that becomes the driving force of what they do.

It sounds kind of glamorous when you think of Angelina Jolie donating millions of dollars to the Lost Boys of Sudan (and dozens of other causes she gives to that I found on her website). But what about you and me? Living our small lives that maybe only a few people will ever know or care about. Isn't our why important too?

Of course it is. That small-town mortician gave the most valuable commodity any of us have to offer: time. Ephesians 5:15 says, "Be very careful, then, how you live—not as unwise but as wise" (NIV).

Be careful how you live. Small, everyday choices can lead to monumental consequences or rewards. Even the smallest decisions we make are all a part of the big why of our lives and the lives of those we touch in ways large and small.

Like when my younger daughter is begging me to throw the Frisbee or play a game of basketball in the driveway, or I receive an invitation to come sit in my teenager's bedroom and listen to her new favorite song—but I have my nose stuck in the computer or I'm working on a song. My first instinct is to say, "I'm busy now" or "Give me a few minutes." (Words that might one day be etched on my tombstone.) When I am cleaning the kitchen for the fourth time that day, I remind myself that one day the house will be tidy and silent and I will be wishing there was a mess to clean up, someone's hair to put up in braids, a Frisbee to toss, a boy band song to listen to, a game of hoops to play in the driveway. It all slips away from us. How we dole out our time is an enormous expression of our why.

A small life can be one of the most beautiful of lives.
Every day.
Ask the question.
Why?

Under a Cloud

I HAVE ALWAYS BEEN ready for the other shoe to drop.

It is common in the South for people to prepare for the worst. In my family, we were always bracing ourselves for the worst, long before Joel Osteen's positivity sermons made us think we should put on a happy face no matter what.

People used to face bad news head-on. Didn't try to make fresh-squeezed orange juice out of those stale, dry oranges that had been in the fridge too long. Sometimes things were how they were and you just called it like it was. You simply didn't have the energy to pretend otherwise.

I ran across a photograph that is a precise example of this behavior.

It is, I imagine, the first photo of us kids taken after the death of our brother Samuel.

I am not sure whose idea it was to capture this moment, but the reality of life is written on our faces. Our dog, Charlie Brown, is in the photo. The only photo that was ever taken of him that I can find. I loved that dog.

It didn't look like any of us had planned to have our photo taken, based on the condition of our clothes and hair. Maybe we were at a flea market and there was a pop-up camera tent and my mom thought it would be a good idea to take a photo.

Of all the pictures in our family album, this one rings most true to me, reflects what was really going on. There are no half smiles or charming poses. We were young enough not to feel the need to pretend. We were comfortable showing our utter disdain for the camera and the man behind the lens, who was probably happy to collect his five dollars and send us on our way with this memorial to the dark cloud that hung over our lives.

It makes me remember what it was like living under that cloud. Wherever we went, we could feel a dark foreboding following us around. And yet even the act of taking that photo was evidence that we were struggling to gather the will to go on. The force to keep life moving forward. Watching and waiting for the day when we outran that dark cloud.

When I think of the years I have battled with fear and anxiety, I can sense the fragile beginning of that journey in this photo.

Somewhere along the way, I started to make the best of things. I stopped letting my feelings show like I did in this photo. I started pretending that everything was okay when there wasn't a doubt that it wasn't. That's when the trouble started. When I started holding it in, like a giant rain cloud gathering water 'til it could no longer hold it in. The truth of my life started pouring out and there was no going back to what had been. I just had to stand there and let it rain on me.

In a world with so much suffering, it is hard to buy the positivity preachers. Maybe they are sincere. But it never reached me. Their words hit me like a crash diet: You think a sudden and extreme change will get you the results you are after. But what we know to be true is, it is the small changes each day, little by little, making better choices for life, that really make a difference over the long haul. We are all walking through life with pain we have to face and wounds that need to heal, lest we become zombies or addicts. One day, with God's help, we can emerge out into the sun with a feeling of gratefulness and an awareness of what others are going through.

It reminds me of a record Beth Neilson Chapman recorded after her husband died after a long and terrible battle with cancer. In her liner notes she said, "There is no way around the pain, only through it and to the other side."

I take a lesson from her words and from this photo. To never pretend that life isn't what it is and more importantly, that God is who He says He is and can do what He says He can do. He isn't afraid of our tears or our honesty or even our rage. He just wants us to be real.

Not long after this photo was taken, our dog, Charlie Brown, was run over by a passing car. Life sometimes deals us a hard blow. Like that passing car, whether Charlie Brown didn't see it coming or thought he could outrun it. There are some things you cannot outrun. You can only see it for what it is and hold on to God through every step.

This is what I wish I had done years ago and what I am trying to do today. A portrait of our lives is hollow and meaningless if it does not speak truth, whatever the truth may be.

You can't always be waiting for the other shoe to drop, either; that's no way to live. It is hard to conceive that God will be there with you to hold the umbrella over you while the rain pours. But over time, you experience the small miracles and you start to see a slice of sunshine finding its way through that dark cloud. It makes you start to believe that one day the world will be different, the cloud will dissipate and float away, and you notice that up above that dark cloud, the sun was shining all along.

What Is Your Story?

THIS MORNING I DID SOMETHING strange as my morning devotional. I spent about an hour reading obituaries.

There is something so potent and jarring about reading someone's final thoughts of the deceased's life—what it was in a nutshell. What was the last word, the last page of the story of that life?

I read several that were incredibly unflattering to the deceased. One obituary said, essentially, that the dead woman was evil; the daughter who had written it, along with her brothers and sisters, hoped that their mother was reaping what she had sown. Wow.

There were many, as you would suspect, that were sweet and honoring, painting wonderful word pictures of loved ones. Some died alone with no living relatives left to write anything. One was about an older lady no one knew very much about—except that she loved cats and fed all the strays in the neighborhood.

As I read these memorials, I wondered what the importance of each of these people was. Why does it matter? Why does our small life in the enormous history of mankind even matter? The only reason I can think is this:

We are each part of a bigger story.

Years ago at the Dove Awards, I remember Brown Bannister, a beloved and revered producer in the Christian music industry, getting up to accept his award for Producer of the Year. What he said has always stuck with me. He said we are each a small part of the great wheel and that the wheel cannot turn and keep turning without all the parts that make it turn.

Whether you call it the great wheel or the Great Story, we are telling a story, God's story. We all have a place in it.

I grew up the daughter of a mother who could make any tent revival evangelist sweat to hold on to his position. She was and is an evangelist at heart. And now I am starting to realize that so am I.

My way of evangelizing might be different from hers or yours, but in my heart, I want to tell someone about the good news. I want to reach out to that friend of mine who cannot figure out why her life is a shambles and the other friend who can't sleep at night for fear of . . . everything.

I want to tell them about Jesus. About how He loves them and is as close as their next breath but somehow, on the wings of it, I fall short and lose my courage.

I don't like to be pushy. I don't like to put people on the spot.

Years ago, I was a part of a Christmas tour for Compassion International with my friends Shawn Groves and Travis Cottrell and the band we all shared.

After the show, we would all eventually make our way back to the tour bus and get ready to drive to the next city.

One night our bass player, Wes, wasn't on the bus. He was usually on the bus fairly early. We were concerned. No one could find him. After a thorough search we waited and prayed that he was okay.

Eventually, there was Wes—smiling so wide as he came up the stairs of the bus. We were all relieved and asked him where he had been.

This was the story he told us.

He went out the back door of the church to make his way around the building to the bus when he saw a man, the church janitor, carrying two large bags of trash out to the Dumpster. When Wes looked at his face, there was something so sad, so forlorn. Wes immediately felt compelled to ask him a single question: "Hey, man, do you know Jesus?"

Wes, being a very easygoing and sweet sort of fellow, stood there patiently as the man began to pour out his heart, telling him the depressing details of his life. He had once been married with a little girl but had messed up, got involved with things he shouldn't have, and had lost them both. He told Wes his life was a disaster and he had no idea how to fix it. That he was such a disappointment to God, how could God ever forgive him for what he had done?

As he and Wes sat there on the curb by the Dumpster in the cold winter night, Wes told the man about Jesus and how

He came to save sinners. That there was nothing too great that Jesus didn't understand. How He had walked among us and knew our struggles and our pain.

Something about what Wes said broke through the barrier and the man sat sobbing and prayed the sinner's prayer with Wes and gave his life to Jesus sitting there beside that Dumpster—all the garbage and shame of his past carried away and washed clean in that one instant.

Suddenly this man had a brand-new story to tell. The story of God's redemption. That He redeems us.

I have always been so inspired by this story. By Wes and his kindness but also by his boldness. More than anything else, I hope that I am learning to seize the moments to hear someone's story and to speak the love and the life of Christ to them. To take the time to do that and not just rush by, trying to get to my next appointment. To my next goal. My, my, my, my.

I have spent too many years consumed by my own story when the point of all this, one day, when the ink on the paper reads *Cindy Morgan Brouwer . . . died.* Let me tell you, as a former hypochondriac, that is a bold thing for me to write down but that's where this is all headed. One day the story that we have set out to live will be done.

What will it say? I hope it will say something about Jesus. His is the story that really matters, because without it, I have no story to tell.

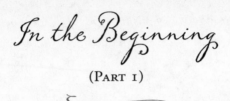

In the Beginning

(PART 1)

In the beginning was the Word,
and the Word was with God, and the Word was God.
(John 1:1 NKJV)

In the beginning God created the heavens and the earth.
The earth was without form, and void;
and darkness was on the face of the deep.
And the Spirit of God was hovering over the face of the waters.
(Genesis 1:1–2 NKJV)

I HAVE ALWAYS LOVED these verses. In the early years of my touring days, I would always read the first two verses of Genesis.

Last year my husband sent a text from the Apple store asking what I would like inscribed on the back of my new matte gold iPad. Immediately, without any thought at all, I answered, "In the beginning was the Word."

I guess I love beginnings. I love the part of a story and of life in general where everything seems endless and wide open and nothing seems impossible. Before the voice of doubt or cynical people tell you that you should just aim low and not get your hopes up.

Even reading the words *the Spirit of God was hovering over the face of the waters* fills me with this grand sense of wonder for what God has in store for each of us. For the life that we have yet to live.

You can probably think back on your life to moments when you felt the Spirit of God hovering over the water. He was there waiting for you to take a step, one that you hadn't planned on; the water is dark with no way to see what lies beneath or above, but this is a step that God knows will lead you to new and wondrous places.

In my life, I remember three such moments.

The first one involved a call to the police for me to be hauled away from church in his police cruiser. I was around seven years old.

We were visiting my grandmother on my mother's side. Her name was Hazel. She lived in Dayton, Ohio, just over the state line from Kentucky, where she had raised my mother and her ten or so siblings. The number was always changing. It was complicated.

Grandma Hazel believed in God, bleach, hair spray, and fried chicken.

Her floors were sparkling like the rest of her house with the faint scent of bleach and lemon wafting through the air. Her hair was teased and perfectly coiffed and sprayed into an early '60s-style bouffant. She wore dresses and panty hose, even to scrub the floors—she was always turned out like a perfect lady. When it came time for dinner, she never took shortcuts, everything was from scratch: From the Southern-style cat-head biscuits (they were the size of a cat's head) to her fried potatoes and fried chicken that simmered slowly in Crisco in her mother's cast-iron skillet, Hazel was a tireless woman of quality. A reputation, no doubt, that my mother found hard to live up to.

It was on this visit to Grandma Hazel's that I had a sleepover at my Aunt Freida's, who lived not too far from Hazel. Frieda's daughters, Anna and Angela (pronounced with a long and somewhat fancy-sounding Awwn-na and Awwwn-gela), very close in age, were my sophisticated city cousins. I was the country-bumpkin cousin.

The invitation was thrown out for me to attend Sunday school with Anna and Angela at the church they attended. At this point in my life, the extent of my experience with church had been the strange charismatic churches my mother attended and the First Baptist church just over the fence of our backyard. My cousins' family—their father was a full-blooded Greek—had attended the Greek Orthodox church since they were babies. I was both terrified and fascinated at the prospect of such an exotic adventure, so we went to bed early with our hair in rollers and caught the church bus together the next morning.

My aunt and uncle chose to stay home, so it was just the city cousins and the country bumpkin riding the Sunday school bus to the Greek Orthodox Church of Dayton, Ohio.

The church was grander than anything I had ever seen. It

had a large and somewhat menacing-looking tall brick facade with a copper dome—and a large gold cross rising out of the dome reaching to the sky.

The bus pulled us around to the back door, where we unloaded and filed inside. I was walking slow, taking it all in. The night before, we had discussed that since my age was in between my cousins—a year older than Anna and a year younger than Angela—we were unsure which class I would be placed in. In the end, Angela thought I would be in Anna's class and Anna thought I would be in Angela's class.

That never even came into play. Because of what happened next.

Angela and Anna were walking up ahead from me as I looked up in awe of the statues of saints and the enormous stained-glass windows as we passed the main sanctuary on the way to the Sunday school class.

That's when I heard it. When I heard the sound that would forever change my life and also reward me with a trip to the woodshed.

It was a sound—sad and mellow and haunting. The notes sounded like someone crying and then another sound—notes that rang out high and joyful and triumphant. It was the sound of the cellist and the violinist practicing in the sanctuary. I banked a hard left and I guess whoever was in charge of unloading the Sunday school bus assumed I knew where I was going. And in a way, I did.

I found a seat toward the back of the church and sat listening to these beautiful instruments as more and more strings and French horns, piano, trumpets and soon an entire orchestra joined in, playing instruments I had never seen or heard before. At once, I felt a whisper inside my heart, like the one I'd heard that day that I walked down the aisle to be baptized.

This whisper said, *This is the way, walk in it.* The Spirit of God had plunged His hand into the dark waters and led me to this moment. I sat there through their entire rehearsal and continued to listen throughout the church service so I could hear them play again.

At some point, I shook myself from the orchestra-induced daze I had been in for two hours and wondered where Anna and Angela were. I would soon find out that the Sunday school bus was long gone and my mother and aunt and grandmother were in an absolute panic, wondering what could have happened to me.

I found a grown-up, tried to explain what had happened, told them my aunt's name, and the next thing you know, I was in the back of a police cruiser, riding to Aunt Frieda's house, *knowing* I was in serious trouble, but somehow feeling like it was totally worth it.

There were tears and hugs and relief and consequences, but in my heart, I knew something monumental had happened to me.

Still today I feel such a sense of tenderness that God looked down upon a simple, unsophisticated child and saw in me something more than what I could see in myself. The promise of what was to come. A diversity of instruments, especially piano and orchestral instruments, have been a staple of the music I have recorded throughout the years.

In the beginning. Such a wonderful place.

Tell Her She's Beautiful

I WAS IN A SONGWRITING APPOINTMENT a little while back with another female artist/writer. A beautiful woman in form and soul. During our appointment, we somehow got on the topic of women and how we can sometimes (mis)treat each other. We discussed the unwritten rules among competitive females when trying to establish who is good, who is better, and who is best.

I am guessing we have all, at one time or another in our lives, run into this.

If high school girls were self-aware enough, they would immediately recognize this as a normal unspoken part of their everyday hallway, locker-room/classroom/bathroom lives.

A few high-school rules:

First, it is a bad idea to have too many (girl)friends who are prettier than you for fear that you will be thought of as the "least prettiest" girl in the crowd.

Second, it is important never to be overheard giving another girl a compliment about her clothing, her makeup, or her hair because in doing so, you are saying that she has superiority over you in this area. This is a vital mistake in keeping up the appearance that you don't care in the least what others think.

Third, whatever you do, never tell another girl she's beautiful. I mean, why would you, for one instant, ever want someone else to feel better about themselves than you do?

I immediately thought of a line spoken by Joy from the television show *My Name Is Earl*, who said, "You need a fat friend to make you feel skinny, a poor friend to make you feel rich, and a dumb friend to make you feel smart."

Ouch. This can't be right. Right?

Last week I met my girlfriend Paige for lunch. Paige is the kind of woman who lights up a room, and you always feel like a better person after being around her.

We met at a little artisan café that we both love with a menu that is constantly changing based on what's in season and local and whatever the chef fancies making. Most would consider it a bohemian/hipster café. Nashville has a thriving art scene, and at this café you can almost always spot someone hot in the indie music scene or a well-known producer, painter, or poet. The waitresses here are stunning. I mean, I think it must be a prerequisite that you can't work there unless you are of exceptional physical beauty. These are young women who could be, are, or are well on their way to being models. It's the kind of place you dress up for, simply because the people there are so darn perfect.

Paige and I sat down and immediately our waitress greeted us.

She had milky white skin, ruby red lips, and ebony hair that Snow White would be jealous of. She was stunning.

Immediately, my friend said to her, "Well, don't you have the most beautiful skin and hair. You are just beautiful." The girl was simultaneously grateful and struck with an equal dose of shyness. I am guessing women aren't always so kind to a girl with such beauty.

I looked across at my friend and thought to myself, *This is it, this woman is the gold standard of how we should treat each other.* We should never be afraid to tell another woman she's beautiful.

I have discussed this with my daughters a few times, particularly when they started school, so it's on my radar. But it is something I am always kicking myself to put into action.

You know how it is. You can be standing there looking at an amazing and gorgeous woman and instead of celebrating her, you are mourning that dessert you ate last night that you can suddenly feel on your waistline. Or you are wishing you'd made time for your devotions this morning, because you were ready to dig in to some good gossip, while your friend just glows with the love of God.

But comparison is the thief of joy. Instead, I want to let other women sharpen my spiritual walk, let them remind me how I could be more instead of getting dragged down into the mire. I want to remember when I am in a position to be the encourager for someone else to *pass it on*, rather than hold it in and wish I had later.

One of my daughters told me about a friend who was very thin but was constantly saying she was fat. The girl's (evil) stepmother apparently tells her on a nightly basis that she is fat. My daughter told the girl how beautiful she was and how she wished she could see herself the way others did. I was so thankful and so proud that she chose to encourage this girl. To try to drown out the evil words that were tearing her down and keeping her from becoming the young woman God has made her to be.

We know there are those out there who will choose to tear down, but I know so many good women who make the choice instead to build up.

I think we have made such a big (unhealthy) deal about looks that we sometimes overlook those people who are just beautiful and glowing in a way that isn't superficial but goes far deeper than any makeup can counterfeit. These ladies need to hear that they are beautiful. From skin to soul. Beauty is broad and far-reaching, and our idea of beauty has become so narrow that I fear we are not helping our fellow sisters live in God's joy, for fear that they don't measure up to shallow standards.

Let's put a cork in that nonsense and have some ice cream every now and then and enjoy life and live out what God has called us to.

I challenge myself and you—yes, you, reading this right now—to remember the last time you told someone else they were beautiful or said "great job" or "you are brilliant" or "thank you for being the amazing woman that you are." If it has been a while, let's try to do that. Maybe even each day, find a woman or a girl or a teenager who needs lifting up, and tell her something good about her that you see, that maybe she can't see.

The feeling inside is so instantly wonderful that I can almost guarantee that you yourself become more radiant just by lifting up someone else with a kind word.

Tell her she's beautiful.

Lead Me to the Rock

WE ALL HAVE MEMORIES of our childhood home. The place that made a permanent mark on our lives. Like the song my friend Tom Douglas wrote, "The House That Built Me," the memories of our childhood home never leave us. Back in the days of childlike faith, before the world found us and jaded us, the time when life seemed to be dripping with hope and wonder.

I remember I was around ten years old when we moved from our home in Harrogate. A lot had happened since my plunge into the baptismal at the church in our backyard: My two cousins, Tammy and Sherry, had become my sisters after their father (my uncle on my mother's side) had died tragically. They had been through so much pain and loss that my parents felt led to bring them from Ohio to Tennessee to become a part of our family. There were dark memories that were difficult to erase from our little white house in Harrogate. Everyone felt it.

So it came as a kind of blessing, a miracle even, that after my siblings had moved away to begin their own lives, my dad happened upon a cabin nestled in a valley that would give us a chance to begin again. It was deep in the woods. A hollow at the end of a dirt road that you would have a hard time finding if someone didn't lead you there.

It was the kind of place where my dad had always dreamed of living, a place that reminded him of his own childhood home in the hills of Kentucky. In this hollow the house was a hand-built, tiny log cabin set down in a valley. When you looked up to the sky you saw a perfect circle of trees. Some locals believed the circle was made by a meteor that fell eons before. There was a large creek that surrounded our property and in the summer it was the place that called to me. The trees made a canopy over the water and offered relief from the southern heat.

I was the youngest, the last one of summer. Mine was the last set of bare feet running across the wood floors.

My relationship with my mother, though, was complicated. She was in the midst of "the change" and I was beginning to go through the rumblings of puberty and the erratic emotions that come along with it. In a way, it is unfair to tell you my side of the story without my mother having a chance to share hers, but I have asked and received permission from her to tell my story, and so I shall.

At that point, a few years past the death of my brother Samuel, she seemed lost, aimless. Reaching and grasping for meaning and purpose in the aftermath of her loss. I was in the midst of my own searching for purpose. Curious about the life that lay ahead of me. I longed for my mother's approval, but it never materialized. I worked hard to impress her, but she never was. I longed to see her smile, to experience joy with her, but instead I lingered with her, in between a state of feeling invisible, being ignored, to feeling her wrath and disappointment.

In these moments, there was a place I used to go. A place where I felt a closeness to God and His creation. Where, it seemed, I could hear Him whisper to me. Where the sound of the running water ran in perfect harmony with His voice. In a part of the creek was a series of small waterfalls. At the bottom of the falls was a rock where the water had smoothed out a perfect seat. I would wade into the deep water in my cutoff shorts and find my place at the bottom of the waterfall. It was up to my neck when I sat down. I would sit and watch the birds dipping their beaks in for a drink. Watch a snake coiled and basking in the sun on a rock at the creek's edge.

Then . . . I could feel a sense of peace. I could see out beyond the misery it seemed my life was at that point. As the years rolled by, summer after summer, I would return to that rock to cry, to pray, to dream, to be filled with the wonder of God. I would go to that rock to seek the solid rock. Like a song my mother used to sing back then: "Lead me to the rock that is higher than I." When life seemed to swirl on sinking sand, I could return to that sure and steady place.

My mother and I have had many conversations about those years of life. I now see, as I try to raise my own daughters, how easily tempers flare. How emotions run away with us. Now I have to wonder if my own girls sometimes feel the way I did back then.

I will never forget one of our conversations about those years. In a moment of painful vulnerability on her part, she asked me to forgive her for not understanding me better and for not being there for me like she knew I needed her to be. Suddenly, some wise words I had once heard came to mind. "Mom, you did the best you could with what you had." Sometimes, that's all we can do.

Maybe you can remember struggles from childhood like this. Do you remember a place from your childhood that called to you? A place where you could more clearly hear the voice of God?

I realize I am still in need of such a place in my life, but life is so busy, and there are so many demands and obligations that it seems to be just one more thing to do. To find the time to seek out that spot. But there is a need. Maybe it is a spot in my front yard under the branches of an old tree or a large rock beside the creek that I spotted in the woods behind our house not too long ago.

Where is that spot for you now? Let's make room in our lives for it, a place where we can hear from God. Where the noise and difficulties of our lives are quieted and we can once again hear Him speak.

The Lost Art of Listening

I DON'T LISTEN very well.

Sometimes my daughters have to call my name two or three times.

"Mom. Mom?"

It is a source of great frustration for them.

"Mom!"

I know they are right. It shouldn't be that way. I get lost in my own world. Thinking about all the things most of us try to juggle every day or my latest stress-out about the week ahead or something I might've said earlier that I regret. I don't listen very well.

Sometimes I think I have forgotten how to listen altogether. One of my favorite writers (and people), Ian Cron, once presented a fascinating seminar on silence. He did an experiment with the audience and asked us to sit in silence for a few minutes. It was a large crowd, maybe five hundred people. We sat there in our cushioned chairs staring around the room, up at the lights, trying to ignore the impulse to check e-mail or our Twitter feed. The first thirty seconds were easy. Sixty seconds . . . no problem. But as we ticked into the third minute it became so strange, awkward, like all this nervous energy in the room might explode. We were all undone by a simple act. Being silent.

I recently made a trip to New York City to watch the opening of a friend's Broadway play. I hopped a cab across town to do a little shopping in Soho and discovered that now when you take a yellow cab, they have a screen built into the back of the front seat, playing commercials a few inches from your face for the entire ride. No longer is there an opportunity to ride in silence, staring out the window at the interesting sights you always see in the city or even striking up a chat with one of New York's colorful cabbies. It has all been taken care of. No more chitchat or idleness, just an endless stream of noise taking up every inch of brain space we have.

It sometimes feels like the silence is slowly being siphoned from our lives whether we want it to go or not—and we don't realize the impact that loss has on our soul. Isn't silence—and being silent—a fundamental part of listening? Isn't listening a major part of functioning in relationships of every kind? What are we losing to marketing efforts—in a cab, a doctor's office, even in restaurants—to gain the convenience of never feeling bored or awkward? I fear the price is greater than we might imagine.

Years ago my friend John Mays was inspired to create a record called *The Lost Art of Listening*. The inspiration came during a trip to Estes Park, Colorado, a trip he and his family took each year for a music seminar held in the Rockies. He remembered a moment when he actually heard the grass crunch beneath his feet as he walked along the hillside looking up at the splendor of the mountains. He couldn't remember the last time he'd been quiet enough to hear such a sound. The record he created was a combination of beautiful piano arrangements with the sounds of nature and life. A rocking chair slowly creaking back and forth, a bird's song, a train whistle. I remember listening to this record when I lived alone and had trouble falling asleep at night. Something about these regular sounds of life filled the silence, it's true, but suddenly I was reminded once again of the beauty and peacefulness of the ordinary everyday sounds of life that don't rob from us but add to us.

Isaiah 30:15 (ESV) says this: "In returning and rest you shall be saved; in quietness and in trust shall be your strength."

In quietness and in trust shall be your strength. Oh, that just feels right, doesn't it? I want to make time in my life for quietness. I want to try an experiment for myself. To sit in the silence at the beginning and end of each day for ten minutes. Just to listen or think or breathe or (even better) to pray. I want to see how difficult it is for me to be silent for that long. Maybe I can stretch it to fifteen, even. Who knows what I might gain by recapturing the lost art of listening?

Whatever Happened to Hollis?

(PART 1)

YEARS AGO I WROTE a story about a man named Hollis. It was a true story.

He was a man who had one dream . . . to be a woman.

He was a fixture in our small town. We lived several miles from any civilization, but whenever we ventured out of the isolation of our log cabin in the hollow to do some shopping, we would see him. There was a mountain between us and town, and we would see him there, pushing his bike with bent rims and flat tires along the side of the narrow road. With the skirt of his dress billowing in the wind and a forlorn look on his face.

My dad would pull over the truck and speak with Hollis about the danger of being on such a curvy and narrow road with a such a small shoulder. His bike was so close to the passing cars. Hollis would give a grateful but sad smile to my dad, and then my dad would load Hollis's bike into the back of the truck and Hollis would get into the cab with us. I was usually in the middle.

I got an up-close look at Hollis then. At his piercing blue eyes as he looked at me briefly. I'd watch the attempt at a shy smile run away from his face before he stared back out the window at the road going by.

As long as I could remember, there was Hollis. Everyone knew him. He was the town freak, the butt of all the cruel jokes—but as much a part of the fabric of the town as the hundred-year-old oak tree that stood by the old gas station. I once saw him with his face pressed up against the glass of a small dress shop on Main Street, with a look of sorrow and a small tear trickling down his tanned skin and two-day stubble. Hollis dreamed of being something he wasn't: a woman.

I will never forget an occasion when my mom had taken me into Woolworth's for a shopping trip for new school clothes; we were in the underwear department, because my mom had detoured from back-to-school shopping to buy a new bra. This in itself was embarrassing enough for a kid of my ten years. When Hollis walked into the room, the embarrassment factor went up several notches.

As my mom stood at the square bra table looking through eighteen-hour this or that, Hollis stepped up, facing her from the other side of the table. I sank down as low as possible with my eyes barely peeking over the edge of the table, in case anyone I knew happened to wander into the small room with us.

My mom was kind of oblivious at first, in her own world, when Hollis cleared his throat and greeted my mom by name. "Hi, Lola. How are you—oh, and hi, Miss Cindy, how are you ladies doing today?" Speaking in a soft voice with just the right amount of southern lilt to make you feel at home and safe.

"Well, hello, Hollis," my mother said back to him. "How are you doing today?"

You see, as I have told you before, my mother was fearless and an on-fire evangelist/preacher. She was also always locked and loaded, aimed and ready for a chance to witness. And obviously, Hollis seemed to be someone, in her opinion, who most definitely needed witnessing to.

They chatted a few minutes about the weather. As their conversation carried on, Hollis started to loosen up and began trying on bras over the top of his ensemble for the day—a plaid shirt and floral skirt. There was no way I could look away now. I was in all the way.

My mother paused for a moment, looked up at Hollis with a smile and an approving nod for his bra selection. "That's a nice color, Hollis."

"Holly, please," he said. "Could you please call me Holly?"

"Oh . . . sure. But I have a question for you, Hollis. I mean Holly . . . Why do you want to be a woman?"

There it was. The million-dollar question most everyone in town had wondered but no one but Lola had had the, umm, guts to ask.

Hollis seemed to consider this and with a sigh he answered, "When I look at you, Lola, a woman so beautiful like all these beautiful women I see every day . . . I don't know, I just want to be beautiful like you. I just want to be beautiful."

My mother looked up at him, holding his gaze for a moment, then she said something that surprised me, maybe more than anything she had ever said before or has said since. "Well, Hollis, Jesus loves you, and He thinks you're beautiful. Don't you ever forget it."

Hollis has never been far from my mind. I have wondered many times what happened to him. I stare at the ceiling sometimes and remember his sad blue eyes and wonder what it would feel like to live out life, as he did, with a sense that you are not the person you want to be.

Maybe we have all felt that way at some point. Maybe not in the same way that Hollis did, but to wonder, *Why don't I feel peace? Why don't I feel complete?*

I wanted to find out whatever happened to Hollis. So I went looking for answers. (To be continued . . .)

Making All Things New

WE SPEND A LOT OF TIME trying to make old things new.

We patch up our old roofs like new, sew up tears in our favorite jeans, take our old leather boots that fit so nice into the shoe repair shop to be re-heeled. There is value in things that have served us well but are getting a little ragged at the edges. They just need a little love and care and . . . *poof!* . . . they are like new. Old things made new.

Last year, I decided that I would not purchase anything new—clothes, shoes, earrings, and so on—from June to June. I looked at my closet and thought, *That's it, I have enough for a while.* I will confess that in the six months since June, I have broken that vow in order to purchase one skirt from Dress Lilly for a photo shoot and a pair of pajamas for fear my husband might leave me if I kept wearing the same set of pj's I had.

So now I stand in my closet and think to myself, *How can I make a new outfit out of the same old clothing?* It is surprising how you can see things differently when you have to.

I see a vintage dress that once belonged to my mother that needs a zipper fixed. A pair of J.Crew jeans that are a little too faded to pass for current and they do fit a little more snug than they did last year . . . ouch. But then as I dig a little deeper I find a vest that was a gift from a friend; it just seemed a little outside of my comfort zone, style-wise, but *hmmm* . . . maybe I should try it. Take the risk to push the boundaries of where I feel comfortable. But who wants to do that? Not me.

A friend of mine called me on the carpet to ask why I broke my vow to buy the new pj's and the skirt. Didn't I already have a skirt? Yes, around six of them. Why wouldn't one of those skirts have worked for the shoot? And why did I have to buy new pajamas? Couldn't I just wear my husband's T-shirts?

Darn those questions that have forced me to look a little deeper into the *why*!

Yet I immediately know the answer. It is rooted in an image of a young chubby girl staring back at me in the mirror. I was the little sister with lots of baby fat still hanging on in middle school. My sister had the body of a calendar girl and when I looked at her, I knew we were different. I knew God had not dealt the cards out evenly in the body beauty department. I am a woman who has birthed two children, traveled and toured the world, recorded eight records, walked the red carpet at the Grammys . . . and still, there it is, this feeling of not being enough. Of not having enough. If I could buy that one more skirt or pair of jeans or an entire new outfit, it will make me feel so good about myself. I will suddenly feel differently about my hips and thighs.

Why can I not be okay with who I am? Completely, I mean. The irony is that I do feel a healthy amount of confidence in many areas of my life, but it's that feeling of being seen as less than perfect, less than . . . I don't know . . . the ultimate woman. Who is the ultimate woman?

The Bible's ultimate woman never worries about her jeans being a little snug or her roots growing out. She was good, au naturel. Up early, making breakfast and weaving clothing and earning money for the household and making her husband proud with the glow in her heart and the strength of her character.

But let's face it, that woman in the Bible was dealing with a little different culture than we are today. Still, the truth of it is jarring. She was not very concerned about herself. Her concerns were for the beauty she was nurturing inside. She was ravishing and she knew it, but it had nothing to do with a twenty-seven-inch waistline.

In Revelation 21 God says, "Behold, I make all things new" (v. 5 NKJV). But don't we have to want Him to make it new before He will? What old pain, old insecurity must we release first? We say we want to be made new, but then that means we have to be willing to expose the areas of our lives that let people see where we are vulnerable. Where we are weak. Where we don't feel so good about ourselves.

A therapist friend once told me it is often more frightening to open yourself up to something new and better than to contend with something old, familiar, and bad . . . because at least with the old stuff, we know what to expect. We fear the unknown.

We get so used to the old things, like those old worn-in jeans and boots, that we aren't even sure if we want to step out into the sunlight of a new world where God has made everything new. And better.

It is our hearts He has to make new. We must trust that we are loved and perfect—because when our hearts are made new, Christ lives within us.

We have simply fooled ourselves into believing the "something new" will fix all the old things we don't like about life and, more importantly, ourselves.

This I know with my mind, but it is working its way to my heart; there is only one "new" thing that will reconcile all of this, and you can't order it from Macy's or Amazon.

God has His own superstore, if you will, full of new insights, peace, and opportunities . . . if we could just throw out the old and make room for the new.

The old things are getting old. One day I hope to be ready, little by little, for God to make it new.

Living Out the Dream

WHEN WE STARTED THIS TOGETHER, I talked about dreams. How we are born with a dream inside us, something that beckons to be realized. Sometimes our life has already been cast in a direction that allows us to follow that path . . . and sometimes not.

I have met so many people over the last two decades who have dreams—to be a teacher, a painter, a songwriter or a singer or a novelist—but life and its responsibilities often allow no time to pursue such a dream. But sometimes I meet someone who managed to work it out, found moments at night or early in the morning or on the weekends to write that novel, record some songs, or even play in a local band or at church. Whether it is on a grand stage or in a small gathering, the call must be answered, it seems; otherwise, we find ourselves feeling like there is a piece of us missing.

I remember a story my dad shared with me when I was around twelve years old and able to appreciate how meaningful it was. It is a story I asked him to tell me many times throughout my life—maybe because it reminded me of his love for our family. As I got older I realized it served as a great reminder to always weigh out the paths we choose to walk in life.

When my dad was a much younger man, he took a trip to Nashville. I think we might have even been still living in the small apartment my dad had built on to the back of his VW repair shop. I was very young, maybe only two years old. He and my mom were a struggling young couple, working long hours. My dad had built his own garage and started his business as a Volkswagen repairman.

Although his business was looking promising, he had a dream inside, something he had always hoped to pursue. So, on a weekend when my mom had taken us kids to our grandmother's house in Ohio, Dad found his moment. He jumped into his VW and drove down to Nashville. He had heard that if you were bold enough, you could walk right in to RCA Records and play a few songs.

At that time, RCA Records was in the back of a television repair shop down on what is now Music Row. My dad rolled into town with his hair slicked back and a 45 rpm record of two of his own songs he had recorded. (One of which, I recall, being titled "My Blue Love.")

There was a man there who shook my dad's hand and welcomed him to the back. When he played the song for the RCA man, the guy loved it. He said he had a feeling about my dad. He told my dad that the man in charge was on a business trip but would return the next day; he wanted my dad to spend the night and come back. In the meantime he invited my dad to come and hang out with him that night at the Opry.

The Grand Ole Opry. A very big deal at the time, as country music was exploding in popularity in America. He told my dad to go grab a hotel room and meet him back there and they'd drive over to the Opry together.

My dad returned to his car and pulled out his wallet. He stared down at the few dollars he had scraped together to pay for gas and a couple of meals. He told me that as he sat there, he started rolling through his mind the scenario of what would actually happen if he were to succeed. There would be travel involved. He had four kids and a new business. How would my mom manage it alone? Would he have to move us to Nashville? Would he have to sell the business he had just started to build? How would he support his family until one of his songs hit it big?

He took a deep breath and returned to the RCA man. He explained his situation. The man felt for him but told him, essentially, "Hey, buddy, that's show business." He said sacrifices had to be made for those who hoped to make it.

My dad understood perfectly what he was saying. He also knew what sacrifice must be made, but one different than the man at RCA might have guessed. My dad thanked him sincerely and got in his car and drove back to our home, not knowing all the life (and even the heartaches) that lay ahead for him.

My dad told me he fully realized that had he made this trip at another time in his life, he most likely would have made a different choice. But his life was already in motion; he had a family to take care of.

So he made a choice. He chose to fix Volkswagens for a living and play with a local band for church revivals and small town functions on weekends. At the end of each day, he returned home to us. At four o'clock I would climb into his lap as he sat in his big green easy chair and we'd watch *Andy Griffith* reruns together.

It is a memory that means more than any gold record hanging on a wall ever could. He was there. Not only was he there, but not for one moment did I ever feel he resented it. He made a choice and lived fully and joyfully in the life he was given and the choice he made. When I think of him, I think of his dream and how his decision to find another way to live out his dream ultimately made it possible, one day, for me to pursue my dream. I guess there is more than one way to "live out the dream." My dad's life was proof of that.

Deep Breaths

THE WILL TO SURVIVE is an underestimated force. Sometimes it would seem it has been buried too deep to reach down and grab hold of—but then, something happens to remind you that you want to live.

Like when you wake at night, as I once did, with the blankets somehow twisted and covering your airway. With a surge of adrenaline you yank the covers off your face and take a deep and desperate breath. You would fight anything or anyone trying to deny you that breath. Even though, moments before, you were totally taking that breath for granted. Like air, like life, we can so easily take important things for granted until something or someone reminds you not to.

Someone who shows you the most powerful moment of living . . .

The moment of dying.

She was a picture of health, my friend Cindy. More than that, though, she was a picture of life. Her flaming red hair, a ready smile, and a quick wit always made you feel energized and comforted all at once in her presence. She wore skirts with cardigans the color of autumn leaves. I always think of her when I see the colors of the fall.

She found love late in life. She had married only five years before her diagnosis of lung cancer. Her husband told me he wondered later if she had had cancer their entire marriage but didn't know it.

There was something about that statement that stayed with me.

Are we all suffering from something we don't realize? Something that keeps us from living the life we had always planned to? Something that will sneak up on us one day and the time we thought was limitless will be running low in our overturned hourglass?

Then we find ourselves reaching down for the will to do battle. To survive. To breathe.

I remember sitting across the table from Cindy days after I heard the news.

She told me about her treatment. She and her husband continued to take walks every day. She told jokes and smiled that dazzling smile, trying to make me feel okay about it all.

Somehow, despite what the doctors were saying, she was hopeful. She told me how her precious mom—Lois, whom I knew well—and her brothers were handling the news. She remained full of life and grace and purpose, even in the face of an imminent outcome. Why did she have such hope? Why not feel robbed by God for such an unfair turn in life? Maybe because she felt the diagnosis had given her a sudden clarity that she might not have been afforded any other way.

I remember one of the last times I saw Cindy, she was still well enough to walk, so we took a stroll in her neighborhood. It was early spring and the flowers were bursting though the dark earth. The trees made a canopy over us as we walked. She breathed through the pain that tried to rob every step she took but she pressed on. We talked about songwriting (she was my publisher for many years); she was mentoring several writers who adored her like the rest of us. As we walked she squeezed my arm, and I had no idea, really, that this would be our last walk, our last talk without anyone else around.

It is turning spring now. It is getting very close to the year anniversary of that walk we took.

As the brown grass begins to surrender to the green life bursting through the earth, I am reminded of something she said to me the last time I saw her. She said that dying gives everything in life perspective. What you can let go of and what you should fight for.

What is more important to fight for than life? I am reminded of a passage in Matthew: "Fear not them which kill the body, but are not able to kill the soul" (10:28 KJV). And in James: "Yet you do not know what tomorrow will bring. What is your life? For you are a mist that appears for a little time and then vanishes" (4:14 ESV).

Even though Cindy's body was wilting, her soul was more alive than it had ever been. She finally understood what her hope was about.

Her hope was not in her health, but in her Healer.

The last time I saw her, we sang hymns. I have some recordings of her singing with her brother and nieces. It was a precious gift to be in the moment and so poignant to listen to now that she is gone.

The will to survive is powerful, but it cannot begin to compare to the power of a life fueled by purpose and the understanding of what is really worth living for.

During one of Cindy's treatments, a radiologist said to her, "You are really sick. I mean, I see this all the time, and you are sicker than most people who come through here, yet you seem so peaceful. What's your secret?"

"Oh, that's simple," she said. "It's just Jesus."

That was it. The sum total of her life, her living, her suffering was a tremendous peace in the midst of it all summed up in three words. *It's just Jesus*. In my mind I can see her smile the day she told me this story. For Cindy, those words were worth fighting for.

That's what it really boils down to. We forget why we're here, why we are fighting each day to survive, to go on. Living only for ourselves and our own ideas of success will *always* leave us gasping for another breath.

Can I ever learn to fight and struggle for a chance to tell someone about the love of Jesus the way I fought for that breath? Do I know what is worth living and surviving and ultimately dying for?

Right now, while I go on breathing in and out, in another place Cindy is taking in a beautiful, full, cleansing breath. Her eyes can see what I can scarcely begin to imagine. She is breathing in the same air as her Savior.

Deep breaths.

Blessings in Disguise

HEARTACHES WE GO THROUGH are often blessings in disguise.

I scarcely think I had a clue of what these words meant when they became a part of the lyric of "How Could I Ask for More" about twenty years ago. But now, as I look back, I know it to be true. You could probably trace a moment of a time in your life when you struggled and suffered a heartache, but in the end it was God's protection or preparation for something more. Something better that you didn't even know how to ask for at the time.

The memory I return to is of the last day of summer on a mattress with rain dripping on my curtainless window outside. I had slept on a mattress the night before. It was the last piece of furniture left in the house. It was moving day.

My eyes were swollen from crying the night before. It was the beginning of my senior year of high school. I had finally found a group of friends whom I connected with—which was saying something, considering I had moved high schools three times.

This move would be my fourth.

It wasn't my dad's fault. I knew that. His eyes seem to brim with tears for me, but the VW repair business had dried up and he had no choice but to venture out and try something new.

He had rented a small house in a small rural town in North Carolina, where we had extended family. There were factory jobs to be had, too, but my dad hoped to build a car repair business there.

I think I cried all the way there. The rain was a perfect backdrop for my mood.

The house wasn't so bad. I had my own room and Dad had bought me a keyboard that would fit nicely into the corner. But there were no friends. I was starting over. Again.

The next day, I got ready with bat-sized butterflies in my stomach. I had been told by my aunt Sue that the school I would be attending had a very sought-after music department and a show choir that performed all over the state. Suddenly, there seemed to be a silver lining in that gray sky. But I couldn't help but think of all my friends back home. They would be having a great time their senior year. And here I was, friendless and afraid.

When I walked into the music room to audition for the choir, I had no idea that this moment would change the path of my life forever. Everyone called the choir teacher Ms. K. She was a classic hippie teacher with a bowl cut, gray hair mixed nicely into her black hair, a quick wit matched by a quick temper, the occasional swear word, and a heart as big as Texas for her students. She invited me to sing a few bars, and I happened to mention that I wrote my own songs. She asked me to play her something, so I sat down at the piano. When I was finished she was in a rush to get ready for the next class but she invited me to come to her class in the afternoon. I wasn't sure why but I agreed.

Later that same day, as I opened the double doors to the music room, I heard her telling the story of the new girl she had just met and I walked in. There must have been a hundred pairs of teenage eyes staring at me. I felt like I might throw up. Ms. K turned and said, "Here she is! Cindy, why don't you play the song you wrote for the class?" I immediately started to sweat and my mouth went dry, but I sat down at the grand piano in the middle of the class with the students surrounding it in a half moon.

I struggled through my song—I was okay, not great—but at the end, they stood and whistled and cheered and the sun appeared in my gray sky. Maybe I had found a home among fellow music lovers with hearts open to a stranger.

I am convinced that the heartache of moving away from what felt comfortable and familiar was what ultimately prepared me for the life and the calling I would follow. Since I didn't have a lot of friends for a while, I spent hours every day in my room writing songs on that little keyboard my dad bought for me. And I was able to learn a great deal about music and performing from the music class and Ms. K, whom I loved so dearly.

I am reminded again and again that the struggles and difficulties we walk through, even failures, are there to prepare us for something else. Something that we could not discover living out our lives in comfort.

Can you recall moments in your life that seemed so painful at the time—but that you now look back on and see as a blessing?

I try to carry the knowledge of what God has done with my past struggles as I look toward the future. I remind myself day by day that God has a beautiful plan for our lives. Sometimes there will be pain and disappointment, but the sun is always shining up above the clouds. A blessing that we cannot see as a blessing yet.

A blessing in disguise.

New Snow

IT IS THE FIRST SNOW. It is early morning, I am sipping on my Earl Grey, and watching as the brown dead leaves of my backyard are covered over in a fresh coat of new snow.

It makes me think of new beginnings, of second chances, and most of all, it makes me think of God's grace and how, like the snow, it can make the world seem new again. I can't help but recall a time when God covered me in the fresh snow of a second chance.

It was at a time when my sister Sam was going through a very dark time, having just gone through a difficult divorce. She was a single mother of four kids working two jobs to keep her head above water.

Two of her daughters were visiting me in Canada for the summer, and as we talked, they told me of some mischief they had been getting into—sneaking out and playing with fireworks and other things spirited teenagers will do. I remember a sense of judgment rising up in me and I called Sam and basically reamed her out for not being aware of what was going on. I then gave her a lecture on parenting and how she could improve her skills.

She told me that I had no idea what it was like to be a single mother and to hold down two jobs and also try to navigate the kids' emotions—not only the emotional roller coaster of being teenagers, but also the emotional devastation that kids suffer from divorce.

I thought she was wrong and that I was right. Our pride often blocks our hearts and our ears from hearing what we don't really want to hear or know. But you know, God has a way of revealing things in His own time.

It was less than a year after this that my husband was required, because of his work, to travel more frequently. Without warning I was facing down weeks without another parent in the house on a regular basis—without someone to tag-team with, someone to give me a break, be the bad guy so I could be the fun mom.

Suddenly, my conversation with my sister came flooding back and I had to laugh. Had God arranged or allowed a scenario just to give me a small glimpse into the difficult task my sister faced? Maybe so.

I felt compelled to call and ask her forgiveness. My sister, from whom I had been estranged since that conversation a year or so earlier, accepted immediately and we had a good long talk and discussed the difficulties of finding the balance of being strong but nurturing mothers.

It was a second chance.

It was a chance to see my sister's life and her struggles with new eyes. To get back my relationship with her after I thought that bridge had been burned. It was the gift of remembering to be merciful.

Blessed are the merciful, for they will be shown mercy. I say this verse to myself whenever I hear of someone's failure or when I see someone participating in something I don't agree with. I want mercy. I want grace. Therefore, I must be willing to give it out if I want to get it back. God loves us too much not to show us where we are missing it.

I once heard Gerald McGinnis, a pastor and one of my mentors, say, "Mercy is not getting what you do deserve, and grace is getting what you don't deserve."

So often God's grace and mercy comes in layers, like the snow. It is beautiful and painful and will ask you to endure something—a season of winter so the spring will seem all the more beautiful. But nothing is as beautiful as that first glimpse of the new snow, and God's grace, which covers our sins and gives us yet another second chance, new eyes and new life.

In the Spirit

AS I SINK INTO THE WARM SPOT of my couch, I breathe in the scent of a cinnamon candle and drink my tea and watch the sprinkling of tiny angels drifting down from the sky, building a small kingdom of white. It is the most wonderful time of the year.

You know the feeling I'm talking about. The time of year when we remember why we are here and what life is all about.

But for some reason, as I look out my window, I am reminded of a Christmas that will always be a painful blemish on that warm feeling . . . and yet serves as a reminder of the moment when I first understood what being in the Christmas Spirit actually meant.

It was my senior year of high school. We had moved from Tennessee to North Carolina to finish off my high school experience with high school number four. A year that began with me in a puddle on the seat of my dad's truck. Tears over leaving the friends I had made. Driving up to the small dismal house with no air-conditioning on a stifling August day. The day before school started. It had rained all the way from Tennessee to North Carolina.

We had moved to North Carolina in hopes that my dad's business would do better there than it had in Tennessee. It didn't. After a few months, Dad was forced to find work back in Tennessee, while also helping my sister, who had just gone through a difficult divorce, also in Tennessee.

This left me in a strange home in a foreign land with my mother.

It wasn't warm and fuzzy.

I was a teenager.

She was a woman of strong opinions and a free tongue with which she expressed them. I, on the other hand, was quiet, with all of my angst and rage bottled up. On occasion I got some release through the writing of a song on my small Casio keyboard in my room, the room with creaky floors and windows that let the cold air in.

Christmas came, and it was left for my mother and me to brave it with each other.

There was no eggnog or Christmas tree. She was not the kind of woman who did that sort of thing. Looking back now, I wonder if she was as discouraged about the turn of our family's fortune as I was.

There was pain.

Pain that crept up in the night and whispered to us and woke us up and told us that nothing was ever going to be all right. Pain that neither of us knew what to do with or how to talk about. I guess most families have it. We chose, I guess, to walk in the pain, rather than to try to put on a nice face, decorate a tree, string some lights, and try to pretend it wasn't there.

My mother was a truth teller. For bad or for good.

Like I said, no warm and fuzzies. Isn't this a great Christmas story so far?

So on the eve of Christmas, I received an invitation to go with my boyfriend (yes, I had one) to his family's house. My mom said it was fine so I went.

I had a great time. A large tree with handmade ornaments stood in the center of the room. Eggnog and sausage balls were served. Gifts were exchanged; Christmas carols were sung. It was an evening that could have been a Hallmark special. The evening was topped off by an enormous diamond-and-sapphire ring that said boyfriend gave to me. (He got a sweater from a discount store.) I had never even seen such an expensive ring, much less imagined owning one.

I was high.

High on eggnog and sausage balls and the feeling of being somewhat acceptable to the likes of proper society. High on being the proud owner of such a ring.

Suddenly, I was fully in the Christmas Spirit. It was a thing to behold. Joy to the world.

As the evening came to an end, my boyfriend drove me home. I walked quietly to the door, thinking my mom might even be surprised and happy to see the gift I'd been given.

As I came to the porch, I caught a glimpse of her through the window.

She was sitting in the corner in one of the two chairs in our living room, mending a shirt.

There was no music. No lights strung across a fireplace. There was no fireplace.

No tree. No holly or mistletoe.

There was only the look of sadness and loneliness stitched onto every inch of her face as she mended the torn seam of that shirt. I saw her. The lifetime of sadness, disappointment. A childhood without trees or merry or eggnog but plenty of other things that no one wanted for Christmas. I saw it all.

It felt as if the Ghost of Christmas Present was giving me a glimpse into her life. Her pain. Her grief.

I fought back the tears that threatened to invade my eyes without a warning.

The Spirit moved me.

I burst into the room, ran over, and gave her a hug, which she received but seemed as surprised by as I was. I showed her the ring I had been given, which impressed her very much.

Then I ran to my room and found a gift someone had given me at school earlier that day and quickly rewrapped it for her.

We sat and talked. We made mac-and-cheese. I found myself trying to engage her in conversation, which she immediately responded to.

The Spirit—and I don't mean the Hallmark Spirit, but rather the Holy Spirit, the Christmas Spirit, if you will—let me see, even feel, a bit of her sorrow. It helped me to stop thinking of myself, of my ring, and to see what I was missing.

In the Spirit, you can see things that flesh and bone cannot.

Since that Christmas, my mother and I have made a slow and steady climb. We are still climbing.

My mother's family ancestry is Jewish, so about fifteen years ago she began attending a messianic congregation. As a messianic Jew, she celebrates Hanukkah instead of Christmas, but we find our way through it all. A menorah on the mantel beside the Christmas tree will usually suffice. My dad, who is now with God, is still with us in our hearts. He loved Christmas and loved to make the house feel like Christmas. It is up to us to do that now.

It is still a work of the Spirit. Every Christmas. Every day.

The more of the flesh I have, the more I keep wanting. It never satisfies.

But just a small taste of the Spirit fills my cup to overflowing.

Like the tiny king all those years ago. He came.

In the flesh.

In the Spirit.

To feel our pain and to remind us that we are not alone.

To give us *the gift* that never leaves us longing.

The Fraud on the Shelf

THIS PAST CHRISTMAS, as I read the lists of their "things hoped for Christmas," I noticed on my youngest daughter Savannah's list was an Elf on the Shelf.

I had seen Instagram photos of my daughter's friend's elves in all sorts of mischievous positions. I mean, these elves could do anything. The possibilities seemed endless. I didn't really get it, but then I listen to NPR and avoid much of mainstream culture as a rule.

It was kind of old news, after all: I think the toy had been out for two years or more when it finally appeared on Savannah's list.

So when I went shopping for Christmas, with the help of the attendant at Target, I was directed by a nice young guy to a retail fixture full of Elves on the Shelf, both boy and girl elves. Since I have two daughters, I decided to get one for each. One boy, one girl.

Fast-forward to the opening of said elves. The girls' eyes were filled with total awe and wonder when they each saw their elves. They had a friend over that evening and a conversation started up—about how "only a grown-up can touch it," and if a kid touches it, the elf loses its magic.

"Oh no!" Olivia chimed in. "I already touched the leg of mine."

"It's okay," I said, "you're fourteen and almost an adult. It probably only counts for true 'kids.'" *What am I saying?*

She seemed comforted by this.

So . . . with some probing, I found out the real deal about the elf but (of course) kept it to myself, and started thinking of how I might sneak into each of their rooms and unleash the supposed "magic" these elves possessed.

But when the guests were gone, my youngest daughter, just eleven years old, said, "My friend told me . . . there is no magic. The parents move it."

First, I entertained a notion of finding her friend and asking her why she found it her place to inform Savannah of this. I mean, it's like saying to a four-year-old that Santa doesn't fly and shimmy down the chimney. The wrapping paper was still lying on the floor and Savannah's hopes of the magical elf were dashed.

Then she did something so brave. She said, "Olivia doesn't know. Let's at least make it magic for her."

I put my arms around her and told her how kind I thought that was of her, and then I felt her sobbing against me. "Oh, sweetie, are you okay? What's wrong?"

That's when she said it. Words I will never forget: "I wanted it to be magic."

Wow.

To think that something you can purchase for $29.95 at Target can be magic is far-fetched at best. But I have so many thoughts on this red-coated fraud and the makers of it.

First, a toy a child can't touch. Isn't that just wrong at its core?

Second, the parents are then brought into the lie that, astonishingly, has taken in loads of middle schoolers and high schoolers who lost belief in Santa back in elementary school.

But what is the deeper issue? I wonder. Is there a part of us that deeply wants to believe in things that seem impossible? You'd better believe it.

I think there is a word for that found in the Bible. I think it's called *faith*.

In a culture that has become so cynical and skeptical, where innocence in some instances is cause for ridicule, there is still a desperate hunger for that sense of belief and wonder and, yes, magic. But where we have been deceived is to believe that it resides in a cloth toy with a blank stare.

It exists. In our hearts. In our prayers. In our belief that God can bring something to life that no one else can—most likely not an elf, but a dream given up on, a disintegrating marriage, a fractured friendship, a lost hope.

"I wanted it to be magic."

The magic is found in the hope Christ has placed in our hearts. The possibilities are endless.

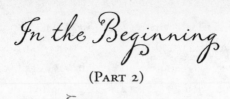

In the Beginning

(PART 2)

THERE WAS A MOMENT when the Spirit spoke to me. I had trouble hearing it at first, just a tiny echo in the back of my head, and then I heard it. Felt it. Knew it.

It was years ago. The summer following my senior year I took a trip to UT (University of Tennessee) to take a meeting with a guidance counselor about enrolling in college. Most of my siblings had gone through some sort of higher learning, all my friends were certainly planning to attend college, and so, I guessed, I would too.

And yet . . . the Spirit.

Not every believer wants to get into a conversation about the Holy Spirit. For some it might be a little too charismatic. Just give us our padded pews and Jesus on flannelgraph, a nice dress for Easter, and we're good.

Arguing about religion or God always seems to divide; it does more damage than good. But no one can argue with your story, the truths you have come to understand about life through your own experiences.

So I have to wonder how different my life would be today if I had not heard the voice of the Spirit—that small whisper or that nagging feeling in the back of your mind that says *Yes, go here* or *No, this isn't the way.*

This was back in the very late '80s when cell phones were the size of a toaster, and only the very rich could afford such a luxury. There was certainly no GPS. It was just me with directions to the guidance counselor's office written on a napkin, with ten bucks for gas for the ninety-minute drive to UT.

The University of Tennessee is an enormous campus, wrought with one-way streets that all look the same. I had been driving around the campus for what seemed like more than an hour. I looked down at my watch and saw that I was already late for my meeting, and I still had no clue how to find this small office in the maze that was UT.

I pulled over and found a parking space under the shade of an enormous oak tree.

I was frustrated and disgusted with my lack of navigational skills. I should have left home two hours earlier. I should have stopped for directions. I could see my future unfolding before me: a life of minimum wage, dead-end jobs. All my friends were already enrolled and had their dorm room decorations picked out and here I was, lost, staring down my life like a black hole. I was the baby of the family. For some reason, that made me feel an enormous amount of pressure to get it right.

Then I started to wonder why I had made such a sudden decision to go to college. All I ever thought of in high school was music. Writing songs and maybe moving to Nashville someday. I had never even thought that seriously about college, and outside of my English literature and music classes, my grades were . . . Well, let's just say my parents were never offered the My-kid's-on-the-honor-roll bumper sticker.

And it occurred to me while I fanned myself with the soggy napkin of failed directions there in the sweltering heat that the only reason I was going to college was because it was what all my other friends were doing.

What if college wasn't for me? What if this whole fiasco of getting lost was God's way of confirming that this was not the path I should take?

I know. It sounds like the easy way out. And maybe it was . . . or maybe not.

I will tell you I would be sad and disappointed if either of my daughters missed out on college because they couldn't find their way to the guidance counselor's office. In the end, though, that journey is theirs to take.

But this I can say for sure: An enormous weight lifted from my shoulders, and I heard a small voice inside say, *Don't worry. Trust in Me.*

Less than a year later I would enter the National Mountain Music Festival contest at Dollywood. There were eight thousand contestants competing for the grand prize.

I would be awarded that grand prize (by Dolly Parton—I have the picture to prove it); sign a contract to perform at Dollywood; meet my friend Kirk Talley (at Dollywood), who introduced me to John Mays, who would later that same year sign me to a record deal.

But much more importantly, I would have a moment in a backstage dressing room at Dollywood, when I heard the Spirit speak to my heart again. It was there I made a promise that I would devote my gifts to God's kingdom, whatever that meant, whatever road it might take me down.

It is a promise I have broken at times, but one I have struggled to keep.

And so, even today, I keep listening for that voice. The one that spoke in the fluid notes of a cello to the little girl in that Greek Orthodox church. The one that spoke to a young, frustrated woman on a college campus. The one that speaks to me now.

Don't worry. Trust in Me.

Photographs of Life

THERE IS A PHOTO of my mother that I remember from an old book of photographs, the kind you pull out on rainy days and Christmas.

In the photo she is standing by a river. Her auburn hair is down and pulled back on the sides; she wears a black skirt past her knees and a white button-up blouse buttoned to the top. In her arms she holds a large white leather-bound King James Bible, close to her breast, as if she is holding on to it for strength, for life. She looks like a missionary about to board a riverboat that will take her somewhere far away to save a life or feed someone hungry. This was the life she said she had always wanted, as a child . . . to be a missionary.

In this photo my mother has a look on her face of sadness. Of regret. In her life there was much cause for sadness and, like most of us, some for regret.

She grew up in the backwoods of Kentucky, the oldest of ten or eleven children. The exact number seemed to change. It was complicated.

The genesis of this photo lies in a story of my mother as a girl, who died in the old shack they lived in. The story went that my aunt Fanny carried my mother, Lola, to an old tree beside the house and, holding her there, prayed a loud and desperate prayer for her life. In her arms, my mother took a deep breath and her life returned.

You know how old family stories are. You hear little bits from the hallway at night when you can't sleep or while you're passing around the fried chicken at the dinner table. And little pieces of the story fall away and you just fill in the blanks with your own version. I have to think that's what happened with this story, because when I finally asked my mom to tell me the details, the reality of the story was very different and quite a bit more remarkable than the story of my remembering.

Sometimes I'm a little nervous to ask my mother too many questions, too many details, for fear my memories will be obliterated by some boring truth—but it seemed important. And so one day while I was frying potatoes in my grandma Hazel's cast-iron skillet and the kids were out in the yard playing, I asked my mother to tell me one more time . . . "Mom, what happened that time when you were a girl and you died?"

A small smile spread at the corners of her mouth as she placed her hands firmly on her round hips and began to recount the story.

"I must have been about two"—I had always thought she was closer to ten—"and I died from having six seizures in a row. Bam, bam, bam, they just kept coming. Finally, my eyes rolled back in my head and Mama got down on the floor crying and screaming. 'No! No! No! Lord, no!' Mama was pregnant with Willard at the time.

"Well, there was some loggers out in the forest who heard

Mama crying. Aunt Fanny was there too. The loggers came running to the house, they came in and saw me lying there. One of them lay his head on my chest and then put his ear over my mouth. He took his hat off and paused and found the words and said, 'I'm so sorry—she's gone.' Tears sprang to his eyes, this kind stranger who didn't know us from Adam. 'She ain't breathing and her heart ain't beating.'

"Mama Hazel let out a scream that would make the demons run and hide. Aunt Fanny ran to a little room we had in the back where we stored the potatoes and strung-up leather britches beans. Aunt Fanny was crying and rocking back and forth and praying with sweat and tears running down her face. 'Jesus, don't You do this!' Mama kept saying 'No! No!' and she massaged and beat my chest and kept saying, 'Don't you die, Lola! Don't you die!'

"As I lay there, a woman appeared in the doorway. She had a beautiful smile and was wearing a long white dress. She knelt down beside me on the other side of Mama and she picked me up in her arms. She looked down into my face with such love. I had never felt such gentle love from a woman before. She walked with me. It was early spring and you could hear the birds singing. It was wonderful. We had an apple orchard in the field beside our house, and she found an apple tree that had a good amount of green leaves on it. It was too early for apples but you could smell the sweetness of the apple blossoms. She sat down with me under that apple tree with her back against the trunk and she prayed and then she would pause and smile at me and stroke my face with her hand. She held me and she prayed. I held on to her and wondered who she was and I wished that she could stay with me always.

"It was then that I opened my eyes and found myself once again lying on the floor in our two-room shack. Mama was bending over me and crying and squeezing me and saying, 'Thank You, Jesus!' Fanny ran in from the back and started to clap her hands and dance around. I was confused and I wondered where the lady in the white dress from the apple tree had gone.

"Later, when everything had settled down, I asked Mama Hazel about the lady and who she was.

"Her face turned white when I asked her, and then she answered, 'Lola, you were lying on the floor the whole time. There was no lady in a white dress . . . but maybe she was your angel.'"

I kept frying potatoes, amazed by the miracle of this story. I watched my mother's face as she remembered this story, but my mind was racing. No wonder she was fond of testifying! She had come back from the grave as a child and then once again as a young woman. (But that is another story altogether.)

My mother's life-after-death experience hid underneath a branch of fear and wrath and unrequited desires until the day, somewhere in the midst of my girlhood, when she decided she would no longer be bound to a life of fear.

Prior to this, my mother's fears, and in some ways, her wrath, were handed down to me. It has been something I have tried to unravel and still today find small strands of the chord within me. Where my mother had no fear of illness or death or snakes or spending the night alone, her fears were rooted in something much more powerful. Her fear was of the consequence of not using the life she had been given for the glory of God. Her calling demanded of her a seemingly impossible scenario, but the fear of not using her second chance at life would not leave her alone. She feared disappointing God. Can you relate?

This might begin to explain why—with the path to become a missionary blocked by her own mother when she was just a teenager—years later, in the 1970s she heard the call to preach. She calls it testifying, but preaching was what it was. Altars at small country churches from Tennessee to Virginia shook from the sound of my mother's calling. A rattlesnake would have been more welcome in some pulpits in the mountains of Appalachia than a female preacher, yet she was undeterred. My mother possessed (and still does) a remarkable singing voice and a striking beauty, which got her the invitation to sing. My mom would sing a little and preach a lot—and while those backwoods preachers steamed in the front row, my mother lived out her calling to spread the word of the gospel.

I find this inspiring in so many ways, terrifying in others.

Our fears can cause us to shrivel or to thrive. In my mom's case, she decided she would not take for granted the second chance she had at life, where, underneath that apple tree, her aunt Fanny's prayers reached the ear of God and her life returned. She would stand against conformity and the disdain of others to live out the calling on her life.

When I think of how my own fears have paralyzed me and sent me on a wild goose chase to root them out, I wonder why it took me so long to face them. It's like walking along the edge of a cliff at night, somehow trusting that the hand of God will be there to catch you if you happen to slip on the rocks. Is there a photograph—one snapshot that encapsulates my life—that one day will remind my own daughters that I didn't let fear hold me back? That my fear didn't stand in the way of the glorious (and sometimes ordinary) living of life?

My mother and her unconventional bravery reminds me to never let fear undermine the life and the calling God has placed on my life. To never look back on life and wish I might have done this or tried that. Think about it. Unlike my mother, you and I might not have a second chance once the golden bowl is smashed.

Are there fears in your life that are keeping you from living out your dreams and passions? Do you still sense the embers of those dreams still burning—but just barely? What old fear will you have to face to blow that ember into a flame?

Don't give up on your dreams. It is never too late to live out the life God has called (and is calling) you to.

He says, "Fear not, for I am with you; be not dismayed, for I am your God; I will strengthen you, I will help you, I will uphold you with my righteous right hand" (Isaiah 41:10 ESV).

This is the life and the day that the Lord has made. Let us live fully in it.

Rice Pudding

These four walls seem ready to give
It's like they know where the weak point is
So I sit and stare
Dirty dishes stacked up in the sink
Speak a word and you're out on the brink of a jagged tear

And you wait and you wonder
And you push against the dark
Every day going under wishing someone knew
The beat of your breaking heart

THESE ARE THE LYRICS to a song for a record I am working on.

Depression has never strayed too far from my doorstep.

My first glimpse of depression came back when I took a trip home to visit my father years ago when I was around nineteen.

He and my mother had moved from North Carolina back to Tennessee and lived in what Southerners would call a "granny house." It had small rooms and ancient wood floors that sloped and creaked when you walked on them. Oh, and the best part? No indoor plumbing. Yes, if the call of nature came in the middle of the night, you grabbed a flashlight and your coat and prayed the coyotes were off chasing a rabbit somewhere.

Did I mention that my family were hillbillies? Oh yes. But this was the kind of place my parents had always dreamed of owning. A return to the simpler life, this little white house was nestled on a beautiful hill overlooking a green valley, like something from a postcard.

I came home one weekend to spend some time with Dad while Mom was in Ohio visiting her mother.

My dad was always a tidy person, though not in the way you might find annoying or unwelcoming. There was always a scattering of books in the living room and work boots at the door. It was comfortable and loose but things were clean and orderly and there was usually something good in the oven for dinner. Whatever house my dad was living in—granny house, outhouse, and all—he always made it feel warm and welcoming.

I think most of us would say food plays a significant role in our memories of home and coming back home. When I think of coming home, I think of my dad's rice pudding. He always made it. It was love in a bowl.

But when I came through the door that wintry December Saturday, there was something different, something . . . off.

There was no rice pudding on the stove or beef stew in the oven. The house felt cold and there were dirty dishes in the sink.

Just as a parent can pick up on small changes in a child that foretell a possible problem, the moment I saw those dirty dishes in the sink, I knew something was up.

As we talked, I kept trying to ask him how he was, what had been going on. He spoke as though everything was normal, but I knew better. He smiled, but his eyes had dark circles underneath them, and he seemed to have lost a few pounds. I called my mom from a telephone in the other room later that evening and told her it might be a good idea for her to cut her visit with her mother short and come home.

Dad needed her.

Now, as I look back, I have my own theory about what happened and why he was depressed.

Even though I had left home a year earlier, since my high school graduation in North Carolina, my parents had moved back to Tennessee into this small house. They were a few hundred miles away from my brother and sisters, who were still back in North Carolina. I lived two hours away in Knoxville, where I was singing at Dollywood and only able to visit on the occasional weekend. Now Mom was in Ohio. My dad had always loved the rolling hills and lush valleys of Tennessee, but now in this little house he recalled memories of a home bursting with the sound of teenagers arguing, and the front door opening and closing as kids came and went. *The TV's too loud, pick up this mess, you're not going to wear that, are you?* All those sounds were replaced by a ticking clock and hours to sit by himself and wonder where all the years went.

I understand this. Sometimes, when my girls are both out for the evening with basketball or choir or archery or Beta club and my husband is away on a business trip, I come home and the house is so still. Immediately I feel covered in a kind of loneliness. I want to turn the TV on. Fill up the silence.

It makes me wonder how in the world I will face life without my kids living within these walls, asking me for ten things at once and making me want to pull my hair out. I try to remind myself in those moments of chaos that one day, like my dad, I will sit and listen to the ticking clock and wonder where the years went. Who will I make rice pudding for then? Rice pudding for one sounds like the most depressing idea I have ever heard.

My dad died suddenly in February of 1999 of a massive heart attack. I never saw it coming.

None of us did. Now, as I think of him, and I look into the eyes of my own children, I know why he didn't tell me what was wrong. He wanted me to fly. Be free. To feel no guilt over going out to live my life and chase my dreams. But, oh, what I would give to go back. To savor more days with my dad. I was so driven by the desire to pursue music that I fear I missed out on lots of beef stews and rice puddings and walks through the woods with him.

My mother came home from Ohio and a few months later my parents decided they would move back to North Carolina to be closer to the new grandchild on the way. No matter how beautiful Tennessee was, it wasn't worth missing out on family.

My brother and sisters lived close by and had years of rice pudding. And, I scheduled as many concerts in North Carolina as humanly possible, and I could always count on that warm smell of vanilla when I walked through the door of my parents' home.

I know what's for dessert tonight.

COVA'S RICE PUDDING

1/2 to 1 cup of white rice
1 box of vanilla pudding (not instant)
Half of a box of lemon pudding (not instant)
1 tsp. vanilla
Dash of cream

Steam 1/2 to 1 cup of white rice.

Make 2 types of pudding (not instant); use a whole box of vanilla and a half box of lemon. Follow the directions on the pudding box.

When both puddings are ready, mix together. Add a teaspoon of real vanilla, the rice, and a dash of cream on top.

Eat warm.

Motherhood

HERE IN THE SOUTH, there has always been a deep reverence for motherhood and the important role it plays out in the world. Country music is brimming over with shout-outs to moms, but as American culture has changed, maybe that has too. There is no one, all-encompassing definition of motherhood these days. And moms themselves morph over time and circumstances.

When I found out I was pregnant with my first daughter I was on a tour. I was into my fourth record with Word Records and had easily spent 80 percent of my adult life up to that point touring. I was gone about 300 days a year, living out of a suitcase, and really having no other life outside of writing songs, making records, doing shows, and packing up to do more shows. It isn't a life for everyone, but it was my life. I toured the entire pregnancy, and honestly, I thought that after I had Olivia, that everything would go back to how it had been before. I would get right back out on the road, hire a nanny, and keep cruising.

Wrong.

What I know now—and what every sane mother knows—is that from the moment you look down into their red faces after they have left the safety of that warm place inside you and are burst into this harsh, bright world, there is *nothing* you would not do, fight, kill, or change for them. It is as if God has been saving a part of your heart that feels a deeper love and a greater emotion than you even knew existed.

A couple of months after Olivia was born, offers starting coming in to take off on a tour, and I starting processing the idea of leaving this tiny creature with someone else. Immediately, I knew my answer. Not a snowball's chance in . . . you get the picture. I knew I would be gone not just for a few hours in the day but for days and very often weeks.

I know lots of artists who have traveled for years with a nanny (or two) in tow and have made it work beautifully. But when Olivia was just a baby, I just didn't think that was a road I wanted to go down. I made a decision to press pause on my life as a touring artist and become a full-time songwriter. Writing songs, and writing in general, was and is actually what I love most.

Once Olivia was out of diapers, our family moved to Los Angeles; we rented a small apartment in Burbank, where I wrote for Warner/Chappell Music. I would brave the traffic and general insanity of LA to go out a few hours a day to write songs and return in time for her afternoon nap. While we were in California, we found out we were pregnant with Savannah, and just like before, all those warm and fierce feelings of protectiveness and love spilled out for my little Savannah. Once again, I was never more sure of the path that I had chosen.

I remember a very poignant conversation I had with a

friend of mine in LA about being a working mother. She and the other single or married-without-kids women looked at me with a suspicious eye. In LA, to be a mother was to knock your worth down several notches. After all, you're not as hot as you were before having a baby. You can't run off anytime you want to do a show at a club when you're a mom. My friend worried that if she became a mother, people in the music business would think less of her.

There were so many women I met in Southern California who had chosen not to have children for the sake of their careers. A fact that still hurts my soul today. Who proclaimed this as truth? Are women viewed differently once they become mothers?

Just a few days ago a friend of my mine posted on her Facebook page. She said it seemed as if being a stay-at-home mother had become something to feel embarrassed about. She felt that because she was not a woman/mother who worked, she wasn't contributing to society anymore. That she was seen as uninteresting and less than a mother who worked.

She also said she had worked in a day care for years, where mothers dropped off their kids at seven in the morning, picked them up at six in the evening, five days a week—and the kids just sat there for a large part of the day, crying for mom. You and I both know there are single moms out there who have no choice but to work, and day care allows them to. And there are some fantastic, nurturing day cares out there . . . But still, it's a sad thought.

When did our culture start making stay-at-home mothers feel as though they are not contributing something of the utmost importance to our society? Why is work outside the home deemed more important than work inside the home? Why do we have to choose?

I have spent the better part of my life as a mother, working for a few days of the week at first and, now that my kids are a bit older, even touring again, but it is still a balance that I am constantly trying to fight for. Sometimes I lose. I happen to believe that I am a better mother—that is, a happier mother—if I am working on a song or a book or a record. To deny all of that would be a difficult thing for me. I feel so grateful to have a career that allows that flexibility, but not every mother has that same option.

At the same time, I have missed games and choir performances and good-night kisses I can't get back.

Do I think I will wish I hadn't one day when they are driving away? Perhaps. Am I doing my best to hold on to a little something for myself while loving every minute of being their mother? Yes.

My dear friend Val had one goal in life, from the time we met shortly after high school graduation: She wanted to be a stay-at-home mother and drive a minivan and homeschool her kids. She is probably one of the wisest and most content people I have ever known. And she is as sure now, with one son in college and another in high school, as she was when they were in diapers that her calling, possibly her greatest calling in life, was to be a mother. She is also an amazing thinker, a voracious reader, volunteers at the hospital, makes her bread from scratch, and is the best friend you could ever ask for.

Our stories are different, but our desire is the same. The calling is the same.

To be good mothers.

For some, the path to being a good mother is to be a working mom. Some who have no children of their own follow the calling in different ways. For others, it is to be a stay-at-home mother. To be there day in, day out. Whatever the case, many women are called to mother.

It is a call that cannot be denied when we feel it, so we do our best to live out the motherhood life the best way we can. It sounds like music on good days and a dirge on others.

Motherhood.

Fearless

IT STARTED WITH a bad breakup. It had become something much worse. I had gone days without eating or sleeping; I heard voices that whispered words of despair. I lay with my face on the rough carpet of my small apartment in Nashville wishing that someone would mercifully come and check me into a hospital and give me an IV with some chemically induced happiness to make the pain go away. To make the darkness dissipate.

Somewhere in the fog, it occurred to me that I was in what evangelicals would call a spiritual battle. Memories of my Pentecostal upbringing came flooding back, but I had no remembrance of how to battle these demons raging around me. I only remembered the fear instilled in me at an early age. Fear that was still hanging on with every claw it could sink into my flesh. Into my mind. Now I felt weak and especially vulnerable. The skeletons of fear in my closet seemed to rattle louder than ever. I spoke scripture aloud into the air, hoping to ward off their attacks with words far greater than my own but the battle raged on.

Somewhere along the way, my healthy respect for God had turned into a deceptive fear. But in this moment, I couldn't tell the difference. I had spent a few years in a certain sect of Pentecostalism that some might today consider a cult. It had found deep roots within me in my early teens. It seemed harmless at the time, but oh, how careful we should be about whom we let speak into our lives.

So I spent my twenties in the grip of paralyzing fear. A bad day was more than just bad. I thought I would *never* get over my broken heart. I would *never* succeed in music. I would not be able to live a life pleasing enough to God.

And I had many bad days, which manifested themselves in different ways.

Early in my career, I became afraid to sing, during one of the busiest touring seasons of my life. The songs were extremely challenging and pitched in very high keys for maximum impact in the studio. And I was singing them live, night after night, after restless nights on moving buses and early morning flights, with days spent talking during interviews and evenings spent breathing in smoke from fog machines in big production shows. If I'd asked any vocal coach, I would have been told to lower the keys, choose only a few moments to challenge my voice, stay inside a comfortable singing range, and so on. But these people did not exist in my world, and I had no real idea of the demands of touring—so I sought no advice.

There were contracts to be fulfilled, band members who had to be paid, promoters who'd spent months promoting a concert, and the expectations were paralyzing for a girl from the woods of Tennessee. My voice was shot and I had a calendar full of concerts. What had I done to bring on such a terrible, overwhelming trial? Yes, the answer came like a hellfire-and-brimstone Sunday morning sermon: I had sinned, and God was taking away my voice to punish me for my sin.

What I didn't realize then was that our thoughts are the key to how we live our lives, and fear can control our thoughts and actions. Ultimately, fear controls our lives.

First John 4:18 (ESV) says, "There is no fear in love, but perfect love casts out fear. For fear has to do with punishment, and whoever fears has not been perfected in love." The irony is, in spite of this, I was so wrapped up in earning my way to a fear-free life, I could not see that it was this very behavior keeping me in the cycle of fear.

So I set about trying to live a sin-free life. I read my Bible constantly. While others were huddled in the lounge of the tour bus watching a comedy, I listened with great disdain to their laughter while I read scriptures softly to myself, hoping God would reward my piety with a healed voice and freedom from fear. But no matter how many Bible verses I read, I did not feel the freedom I so desperately craved.

I became convinced that vanity was to blame for the sick feeling of fear that was my constant companion, so I made it a regular practice (for probably two years) to cover every mirror I encountered. At home, or the moment I entered a hotel room, I would cover the mirrors. I allowed myself only a small compact mirror to apply my makeup, but still the fear would not go away.

Then I believed that selfishness was to blame for my malady. If I were less selfish, surely God would look down and see my good works and reward me with blessings of happiness. So I began to volunteer at the hospital on the few days I had at home. Visiting the sick did open my eyes to the suffering of others; for a moment the hundred-pound weight on my chest was lifted and I felt free, until I left the hospital and was once again faced with my own shortcomings as a person, as a Christian.

My voice made a full recovery because I eventually got enough rest. But I lived with this feeling for so long that I almost grew used to the weight. I recorded five records and performed in front of tens of thousands of people while carrying around this sick feeing in the pit of my stomach. I got married, had children, and still, there it was, always waiting for me, an awful fear that would not relent. I would watch my children laughing and playing and wonder what it would feel like to be free, to be at ease.

In Alberta, Canada, where we live in the summer, I had a neighbor, Donna, who was a woman of deep faith. I spoke about some of my struggles and beliefs about my struggles and spiritual shortcomings with her. A few mornings later, Donna appeared at my door with a plate of banana-nut muffins and a question.

She said to me, "I was praying for you this morning and a question occurred to me. I have to think the question was from God."

"What question is that?" I asked.

"What is the root?" she said. "What is at the root of your fear?"

It was the single most important question anyone had ever asked me.

Donna prayed with me and left me with her muffins and the question I was suddenly burning to find the answer for.

So I put on my gardening gloves and began my daily weeding in our enormous garden. There are always lots of weeds to be pulled. And in that part of the world, there are thistles that grow in your flower beds and sidewalks and up the cracks of your porch and assault your bare feet in the soft grass of your yard.

I have plenty of experience with weeding. Everyone knows that when you weed, it is best to pull up the weeds from the root.

That day I got a good hold on a impressively large thistle. I started to pull. Thistles, if you have ever seen them, are covered in vicious thorns, razor sharp and needle thin. You can only pull up a thistle if you are wearing leather work gloves; it isn't a job for bright-colored sissy gardening gloves. I stood and began to battle the giant thistle. There must have been several feet of a root buried underground.

My mind raced, considering what lay beneath the surface, feeding the fear monster that had haunted me all these years. Like the thistle root I was pulling on.

What was at the root? What was feeding my fear?

What razor-sharp thorns must I face to conquer this monster?

To answer this question, I had to go back. Back to the women who came before me.

My mother's fears. My grandmother's, and her mother's before her. I had heard the tragic stories of loss and struggle. The stories of a mother burying children and abusive men and no one to come to the rescue. No food to feed the children, no fire to ward off the cold. I felt the chains of fear rattle behind me. The root seemed to go deeper down than I ever imagined.

What was my greatest fear that fueled everything else?

Trust.

The word came like a thorn jabbing into soft flesh.

I didn't trust.

Who didn't I trust?

The answer came as the final inches of the root released and I went tumbling backward.

God.

There had been great loss and disappointment in the lives of the women before me and the cumulative effect seemed overwhelming. Were the tragic things that happened to them due to their sin? Their unbelief or disobedience? These were the kinds of things I was raised to believe. The way to please God and avoid these tragic things, I had been taught, was simple: I had to be sinless.

Otherwise, God could not be trusted to give me good things. Protect me. That was clearly up to me.

I didn't trust that He would take care of me. Or my family.

I wanted God to guarantee that my life would be a good life, without pain or suffering or struggle.

Later that day, after the thistles had been thrown into the fire, Sigmund and I sat by our pond and watched our small girls throwing rocks into the water. I sat perched on the edge of my seat, nervous that at any moment, one of the girls could fall in the water and drown. Fear had now found its way into my parenting.

The look on my husband's face was an exact opposite of mine: a sweet smile, joy, a contentment to watch the girls discover small ants crawling along the ground, to dip their toes in the water.

I asked him, "Aren't you nervous they might fall in?" Wringing my hands.

He answered, "No, because if they fall in, I'll go in after them."

There it was. He knew he had the goods to rescue them. In the process of discovering nature and water and the great big world, the girls might face some difficulties, but Sigmund would always be there when they needed him. My father had been the same.

And I wondered . . . if the Bible says God is our loving Father, even though He doesn't promise to keep us from all the struggles of life, ultimately—like Sigmund and the girls—isn't He always there for us? Will He leave us or forsake us?

That voice I heard in my small apartment with my face on the carpet, that voice said God would not be there, that He would abandon me in my hour of need, and I would be on my own. But I saw on Sigmund's face and the girls' faces the simple truth I had been looking for.

I just had to trust.

That night, I thought of my daughters and the road before them. I knew from my own life that there would be bumps on the road I could not shelter them from. It occurred to me that even though I prayed a lot and read my Bible for hours a day, it had always been about what I wanted God to solve for my life. But, like those fleeting moments of freedom when I visited the sick, maybe it wasn't about me.

I asked God that night to help me surrender my fears and my distrust. Like the man in Mark: "Lord, I believe; help my unbelief" (9:24 NKJV).

I could not turn back time and retrieve the years I had lost, but I could make certain that I didn't let fear rob another single moment of this life I had been given to live.

Each day I try to remember. It isn't about me. Like the prayer we often pray:

Our Father, which art in heaven,

Hallowed be thy name.

Thy kingdom come,

Thy will be done

in earth, as it is in heaven . . .

Are there fears in your life that have kept you from living out the life God has called you to?

Are you able to enjoy life without fear trying to take over?

Are there struggles that you find difficult to surrender to God?

He is waiting there for you, like He was for me, a Father watching over. Ready for that moment when you need Him to come to the rescue.

But He cannot rescue us if we don't accept His help.

Help us, Lord, to ask for Your help so that we can use our lives to make Your kingdom come, Your will be done.

To be fearless for Your cause.

Fearless.

I love the sound of that word.

What Oprah Said

~

SOMETIMES I THINK about what Oprah said.

Back in the days when we all sat around waiting for four o'clock so we could once again catch the drops of golden knowledge and wisdom that fell from the lips of her brilliant peach lips (she wore peach lip gloss a lot, don't ask me why I remember this).

Yes, when my girls were little I would often save my laundry for the Oprah hour and stand with five loads of laundry on the bed and fold and sigh and drink it all in.

Back before she got all New Age on us, she used to say some pretty profound things. One such thing has stuck with me, lo, these ten years later.

I have no idea if Oprah said it first or if someone else did, but it makes a lot of sense to me: *You can have it all, you just can't have it all at the same time.*

Our husbands, our kids, our money, our time . . . why can't we have it all? I have thought about this so much through the years. You know, sometimes you meet someone or have a friend and you think to yourself, *Man, she has it all together—* but in reality, does anyone really have it all together? Does anyone have it all . . . all of the time?

There is always a price to pay for our decisions. For what we give ourselves to. A trade-off. Balance is the ongoing struggle for most of us. Trying to make time for everything.

I struggle with saying no. I have for years. Part of it is that there are so many things I am interested in and don't want to miss out on, but how do we do it all . . . all at the same time?

Was Oprah right?

I read somewhere that a crucial key to success is to focus on one thing that you're really good at, and you will succeed. Now that one thing could have many facets to it. Take motherhood—being a taxi service for activities, being a good listener, doing crafts, helping with homework, housework, being a short-order chef, decorating your home, volunteering at the school . . . I mean, that sounds like a pretty full life, and a complex one at that.

Add to that a job outside the home and a fairly organized working mother can still make room for these things but in smaller doses. The house might not be as clean (unless you can afford a maid or your kids are awesome at helping clean). You might become an expert at Crock-Pot recipes (possibly one of the greatest inventions besides the smartphone).

Many parents have figured out how to balance work and home life. It is something we humans have been working on for centuries. I know many dads in our community who somehow manage to volunteer as a baseball or basketball coach while holding down a full-time job. I know moms who work but always manage to be there for that field trip, or send a hot meal to a friend in need, or even make time to volunteer at school and are always at the stands for their kids' games. Most of these parents do not live in grand houses or drive expensive cars but they are always there, somehow making it all work. They are heroes without capes.

I have to believe at some point in their lives, they made family a priority and the job had to work within that.

But so many other things ask for our attention—being a Sunday school teacher, volunteering, having a weekly night out with the girls (who has time for this?). Taking on that one extra shift at work because you're saving up for a vacation. That one more episode of *Downton Abbey* that you just cannot turn off.

I have a friend who was what most people would consider a workaholic. This woman could hang with the guys and work them all under the table; really, she could outwork anyone I knew. Brilliant, the valedictorian of her high school and college graduating class. Her house was spotless, her closet organized, her bills paid on time, her savings account nice and full . . . and then something happened. She got married. And then something else happened. She had kids.

I had coffee with her when the kids were still toddlers. She had entered the workforce again but she confided in me that she had discovered how unhealthy her life had been before, how one-sided it was. To her, the most important thing in life was climbing the ladder to success. She knew everyone expected her to be the same over-the-top driven person she was before. But now, "Everything has changed." She wonders if any of those executives she worked with ever saw their families. If they missed the baseball games and the dance recitals or—at the very least—the evening meal with the family. They worked late and very often went out to socialize with clients after the workday. This was a very important part of climbing to the top. You have to be willing to make *the job* number one. Almost all of those people she knew are now divorced and have moved on to second and third marriages.

I wonder to myself, are these the people who think you can have it all, all at the same time?

There are sacrifices to be made, but where do we make them?

There is a scripture that always comes to mind. "Seek ye first the kingdom of God . . . and all these things shall be added unto you" (Matthew 6:33 KJV).

God has called us to be good stewards over what we have been given. Isn't family a gift? Aren't children the most valuable of all our earthly gifts?

Seek ye first . . .

What we don't want is to ever look back and see that we never really went deep with anything. That we just skimmed the surface with everything in life but never really gave ourselves completely to anything.

The good things in life . . . faith, church, family, friends . . . how can we have it all . . . all at the same time? We will never look back and wish that we had worked more or owned more. We will wish for the things most precious.

Instead of wishing for them, let's just enjoy them now . . . while we have it all.

Pigtails and Wonder

THIS PAST JANUARY, I was saddened to hear news about an actress who marked not only much of my childhood but of both my daughters' childhoods with a sense of innocence and a kind of otherworldly quality.

I will tell you her name in a moment. First, I will take you back to a plane ride I took, years before I was a mother or even a wife.

I was on one of those really small planes, flying into a small airport in Florida. It could not have held more than twelve people. We were all quite close together, trying to create space and privacy where there was none to be had.

I noticed the woman across from me leaning her head against the window. She had blond hair, worn down but gathered into loose pigtails on each side. Her face was sweet and serene. The fight attendant came by, and the woman looked over at me, possibly aware of my staring. There was something so familiar about her. "Hello." Small plane. "Yes." Very small. Her voice was very soft and her eyes were kind.

I started telling her that the smallest plane I had been on was one that seated four. It made this seem like a jet. She laughed and we started talking about traveling and I asked her if she was from Florida. "No, just attending a conference."

Hmm. That's cool. What kind of conference? "A Christian conference for women."

"I am a Christian," I said. "Who is speaking? What made you want to attend?"

"Well, actually, *I* am speaking."

"Oh" (feeling stupid), "how exciting!" I reached out my hand. "I am Cindy Morgan. What is your name?"

"Donna . . . Douglas."

Donna Douglas, Donna Douglas . . . hold on . . . "Are you Elly May?"

"Yes." She drooped her head a bit.

So went the day I met Elly May Clampett on a plane.

When Elly May appeared on screen, she was always accompanied by classical guitar made to sound like the music of harp strings and angels. She was usually holding some wild animal, which was as tame as a kitten for her. Elly was magical. I know that in reality the animals were trained—but who could deny her enigmatic way on-screen, her delightful innocence that made you want to go out and purchase a pair of jeans and a button-up shirt and tie a rope through your belt loops?

This was all I could think of when I heard the news on New Year's Day 2015, that Donna "Elly May" Douglas had passed on at age eighty-two. It was like a little light had gone out in my heart, a little magic had been drained out of my childhood.

Magic. That is the topic.

The word *magic* has a very negative association with us Christians, especially (we) Evangelicals. Yes, I would consider myself an evangelist at heart. You cannot be raised by a female Pentecostal preacher and not have an evangelist inside of you. From the womb I listened to her thundering sermons from couches, at kitchen tables, and in pulpits of small Southern country churches. No doubt she might have even preached on the evils of sorcery. Or, as it is sometimes referred to—magic.

That word—*magic*—has such power, such a beautiful conjuring of imagination associated with it, but we have, somewhere along the way, decided that magic is bad.

I hasten to agree that all things related to the occult, witchcraft, and the dark world are unequivocally dangerous and bad and should be avoided at all costs. Ask my kids: I am one of those fanatical parents who would not allow my children to watch or read Harry Potter for fear of confusion about good and bad wizards. But the Chronicles of Narnia magic, in my opinion, was of a completely different source, and those books and movies are beloved in our home. In C. S. Lewis's books, he differentiates between the dark magic and the deep magic. These are two very different things, but Aslan refuses to surrender the word *magic* to only the dark use of it. I am not talking about the fantasy of Santa Claus or the Easter Bunny, but things much deeper and more powerful. Something that we cannot at any cost surrender.

A sense of . . . wonder.

Magic is wonder.

Magic is the belief in things that seem impossible, yet possible.

I am reminded of the scripture in Matthew 19:26: "With men this is impossible, but with God all things are possible" (NKJV).

This morning I read (in John 11:1–44) about Lazarus being raised from the tomb, appearing at the mouth of the grave still wearing his graveclothes and, no doubt, scarcely able to walk. Surely those present were dazzled into a state of wonder, a state of utter disbelief—save that *all those standing with them saw it too.*

Have we lost our ability as people to believe in things that seem impossible? I have a relative, with whom I have shared many enjoyable cups of tea and conversation, who believes that healing through prayer (and not through a physician) is something no longer possible today. That healing ceased with the apostles during the first generation of Christianity—as if the imparted gift of the Spirit was not passed on to future believers. As if Christianity is a diluted version of the once-pure thing.

But doesn't this stand against everything we are taught as believers? Aren't we called to have faith in "the substance of things hoped for, the evidence of things not seen" (Hebrews 11:1 NKJV)? And I ask you, doesn't this sense of wonder and the absence of skepticism have a profound impact on our everyday lives? On the quality of our dreams and our dreaming and what we might venture to try? To believe?

Like that part of me as a child—and now my own beautiful daughters—who wanted to believe that a young girl in pigtails could tame raccoons and wild skunks with a smile and a ride on her shoulder.

I don't want to lose the wonder. The belief in things that seem impossible.

I want to believe. Do you?

Comfort

THE POWER OF A COMFORTING friend or family member is something we cannot fully appreciate—until we have lost something so great and the ache of grief is so deep that we find ourselves, as never before, as much in need of it as we are for air.

I will never forget such a moment in my own life. My husband and I were on a tour together, during which he read excerpts from his book *The Weeping Chamber* intermingled with songs from a record of mine (*The Loving Kind*) inspired by the last eight days of the life of Christ.

Ironically, we were in Corpus Christi, Texas; the name of that town is Latin for the "body of Christ." I recall a moment that night when I had a sense of something otherwordly, like I had brushed up against an angel's wings.

The next morning, my husband woke up early, having scouted out a local golf course where he could play a few holes before we headed off to our next concert. I slept in but was awakened by the hotel phone ringing. It was my manager, who said he had received a message from my sister and that I needed to call home. I tried everyone but could get no one on the phone, so I called my aunt Doris, who lived only a few miles from my parents' house in Kentucky.

It was her voice that told me what I did not want to hear; in her soft voice, through her own tears, she told me that my father had passed away. The night before, maybe; they couldn't be sure. Maybe that moment when I felt the brush of an angel's wings? Maybe that was my father saying good-bye. My mind raced and I couldn't quite take in what was happening.

During the long journey from Corpus Christi to a small cabin in the woods of Kentucky, I remember feeling like the joy had gone out of living. My father, the most dear and cher-ished friend of my life, was gone. If ever there was a need for comfort, it was then.

During the days following my father's death, there was much to be done. Planning the ceremony, dealing with fam-ily from out of town, waiting for the coroner's report, which confirmed that my father had died of a massive heart attack. I remember feeling so restless and angry. Why would God take him from us? What good could it do? *We needed him more.* My aunt Doris walked through each step of the process with us: the funeral arrangements, the visitation, the funeral itself, the burial, and even during those painful days afterward being present with my mom. She was just *there*.

I remember asking Aunt Doris if we were keeping her from something she needed to do. To me, this was a logical question because I, like most of the people I worked with, was ruled by the rush and panic of having to go, go, go in order to feel like I was doing enough. But Aunt Doris wasn't ruled by the rush and panic. She looked at me with the most kind and serene of faces and said, "This *is* what I need to do. I need to just be here with you."

Her quiet comfort to our family was such a gift. One I am not sure how to ever repay, except to offer someone else in need that same comfort. It reminds me of the Beatitude "Blessed are those who mourn, for they will be comforted" (Matthew 5:4 NIV).

Are we a part of that comfort? Is a part of our calling in this life to walk alongside those who are in need? There are those who cannot express what they need, but somehow, if we are listening (there's that word again) to the Spirit, we will know how to be a comfort. Up until my father's death, I had no understanding of the value of this.

But I fear that I am not like my aunt. I am the rusher, the squeezer, the person who has a hard time saying no, always overcommitted, always victimized by what Charles Hummel called "the tyranny of the urgent." I want to change that. *Lord, help me to change.*

Have you ever been an Aunt Doris to someone? Is there someone in your life who needs comfort? Do you recall when someone has brought comfort to you during a season when you needed it the most? Let us open our eyes and hearts and be the hands, the feet, and the comfort of Christ, even in the simplest of ways. Let us make room in our lives for comfort. Room to receive and to give.

Bows and Arrows

MOTHERS CAST A LONG SHADOW.

A friend of mine said this at my kitchen table over a bowl of soup and a discussion about her teenage daughters, struggling to find their own identity in the very impressive shadow of this woman before me. Mothers cast a long shadow. I know this is true. I know it as a daughter, but even more, I know it as a mother.

There is that moment when they let go of your hand and begin trying to outrun the shadow we cast before them. I say *we* to try to loop you into my shadow of guilt. The guilty do like some company.

I try to keep my shadow at bay, but it is always barging in and suggesting to my daughters what they should wear, how they can fix their hair (or even better, let me fix it!), more efficient ways to study, how neat their rooms should be. I have a hard time making my shadow shut up. Know what I mean?

Two summers ago, we were walking through the meadow in Canada. It was late summer, the light floating down golden at the end of the day as it cast a magical spell over the world. Over our meadow. The tall grass bent against the wind and the girls ran ahead of Sigmund and me.

Olivia was freshly twelve. Savannah still close to my apron at nine.

Olivia was branching out. Asking questions. Questioning life and creation and wondering about boys and death and if the still baby rabbit Daddy said suddenly came to life and hopped away into the tall grass (when she was ten) really died and Dad just didn't have the heart to tell her.

She was outrunning the shadow I cast for her, and I hated it and rejoiced for it all at once.

As she and Savannah ran ahead of us that day, the sun cast shadows and behind Olivia I could see the long lines of her legs that seemed as tall as mountains, and in that instant I knew that she was less mine and more hers. Her days of castles and imaginary dragons were coming to an end. Like Puff and Jackie Paper, there must be a time when imaginary things are put away, stored neatly in a box in the attic that you return to on Christmas and rainy days.

I wondered how soon I would lose my grasp on her. If she would no longer need me to brush her hair or tuck her in. How long would it take for her not to need me anymore? Would Savannah be close behind?

Do you notice I am having a hard time making this about my daughters instead of how it is impacting me? Stupid shadow.

In Psalm 127:3–4 Solomon writes that children are like arrows and parents are like bows from which they are thrust out into life. This is what we know is meant to happen, but how do we get over that creaking sound of our heart breaking in two as we try to pry loose the vise grip we have on the bow in order to let the arrow fly? It's so hard to let the shadow run free away from you with wild and glorious abandon.

It is ironic, I think, that Olivia took up archery this year. I remember the first time I saw her draw her bow back with such grace and let her arrow fly to its mark. She was mesmerizing.

I want to savor every walk in the meadow, every bedside prayer, every late-night walk through our neighborhood in our pajamas, every fight over who is taller (she is).

It is happening. She is building her own shadow; it belongs only to her and to God. Savannah isn't far behind.

When the time comes, I pray for God's grace to overtake my own shadow and rest in the shadow of His mighty wings.

Whatever Happened to Hollis?

(PART 2)

Hollis D. Moore
Birth: June 15, 1949
Death: April 16, 2011

HE WAS BORN IN SUMMER and died in spring. Greeted by the heat of the blistering Southern sun and cradled to the grave by spring showers and Easter buds.

It was difficult to find anything in writing about either the life or the death of Hollis. The first obituary I found simply said his name, where he lived, and the dates of his birth and death. It makes you wonder who is actually responsible for writing obituaries, this last memorial to someone's life.

It is a grave disappointment to read such a hollow tribute after finding out what I did about Hollis by talking with those who knew him long and best. I hope this will be his last memorial and not the two lines in a small corner of a local paper that someone might have used to line a garbage pail and probably never read.

I had no idea what I would learn when I went searching

for what happened to my friend Hollis. I feel strange and maybe even somewhat dishonest calling him a friend, since he probably wouldn't have remembered me had I walked up to him on the street as an adult. I guess I feel he was a friend for what he gave me as a child—a look at the world beyond my own. Hollis was a mystery, one that I pondered as a child and for lo, these many years into womanhood.

Through newspaper articles, Internet searches, numerous e-mails and phone calls, talking to friends who knew Hollis from childhood, and even a return trip to the town of my childhood, I found tiny scraps of information, small pieces of a puzzle, but I still couldn't quite make out the whole picture, the real story about whatever happened to Hollis. It wasn't until I veered off the main highways and wandered onto the back roads to find the people who really knew Hollis that I could put the puzzle together. Folks who spent hours and months and years seeing him every day or so were able to tell me the true story of his life.

All these years I thought the only thing interesting about Hollis was that he wanted to be a woman, but nothing could be further from that truth. I found it strange—even though we were separated by years of age difference—that much of the early years of Hollis's life and mine followed a similar course.

Hollis spent his childhood in a tiny placed called Tiprell, just a short piece from the beautiful historic valley of Cumberland Gap. He had five brothers, one who died as an infant.

Hollis was the second oldest brother. He attended Ellen Myers Elementary School, as I would also, years later. As far as I can tell he went on to H. Y. Livesay Middle School, which I also attended. But by the time he reached high school, Hollis found himself in a world he simply could not fit in to.

Exactly when Hollis's desire to be female came into play remains a mystery. In those days, such things were politely avoided, not discussed. It appears that he left high school around his sophomore year. So began the familiar sight of him pushing or riding his bicycle from Cumberland Gap across the curvy narrow mountain road over into Kentucky.

If I close my eyes I can see the sign to Cudjo's Cave, which was one of the only tourist attractions in our area. Across the road from the cave was a tiny store with worn wooden floors and a rickety sign, where you bought your tickets to the caverns. I remember taking a field trip there with my class in elementary school. The tiny store was also where my dad went to buy my grandpa Barney's unfiltered Pall Mall cigarettes. It was the only place you could buy them and I was always terrified that God might one day strike us dead for shopping in a store that sold beer *and* cigarettes, but I was even more afraid to get up enough speed to pull back onto the narrow two-lane road, for fear that an oncoming car would send us over the edge. There was no guardrail, so we'd tumble right down the steep cliff that overlooked the valley of Cumberland Gap.

This was the road young Hollis rode his bike on. No doubt this was why my father always stopped to pick him up.

Hollis was what most would have called a wanderer, a loner. In good weather, in his teen years, back when his mama still had the farm, Hollis hung out with a group of friends who had all known each other from childhood. They would camp by the river, catching fish for dinner, somehow surviving without a job of any kind. Hollis was one of the fortunate ones who had a place to go on cold nights.

In the winter, this band of his friends would commit a small crime, bust a window or create a disturbance in order to be arrested so they would have somewhere warm to be in the winter with three square meals a day. While his mother still lived, Hollis was able to live with her and his four brothers.

As Hollis grew older, he stopped wearing dresses and began wearing flamboyant tops (sometimes from the women's department) and sunglasses that put you in mind of old Hollywood stars. Since he had always asked to be called Holly, the natural next step was to call him Hollywood, and for a few years in his early adult life, that's what folks called him. Hollywood of Cumberland Gap.

A few years later Hollis's mother passed and his four brothers moved away one by one. But Hollis remained in the town he knew.

He was known to visit the Roses Shopping Center across the mountain in Middlesboro. A sweet lady named Geri from Cumberland Gap told me, "They would pay Hollis a little something to come play the organs and pianos they were trying to sell in the main area of Roses." Apparently, Hollis was a bit of a musical genius and could play any tune that a passerby might request. He would say, "I think I remember that," and then after taking a minute to learn it, would commence to playing the requested song, throwing his head back as if he were playing at Carnegie Hall. He would also sing along if he knew the words, letting his large voice shake the bulbs out of the chandeliers.

One very close friend of his, Johnny, told me Hollis was an accomplished artist. Over the years the walls of Junior's Car Shop in Harrogate had become an unofficial art gallery for Hollis's drawings. Men waiting to get their cars fixed and locals alike enjoyed hanging out to watch Hollis sketch on the walls, wondering where someone so unschooled and in many ways, uncared for, begot such talent. He loved to draw monsters and comic book heroes. Johnny said, "He could draw anything but he had to want to draw it." He was once given watercolors by John, the owner of the general store in Cumberland Gap, and commissioned to draw the landscape of Cumberland Gap, but Hollis came back with a sketch of a black arch that was his rendering of what he called "the Tunnel"—known to all locals and especially those who lived along the railroad tracks in Cumberland Gap. There was no fencing him in or tying him down or curtailing his talents into something marketable. He did as he liked and created when the mood hit him, and that was it.

In my memories of him, I recall someone somber and sad. Someone who seemed lost. Maybe I felt lost too. Maybe that was why he intrigued me so. I am not sure why Hollis was the way he was. Although I have my own ideas why *I* felt so lost back then.

While I was working on this story, my family took a trip down to Gulf Shores, Alabama. I walked along the beach as you always do, looking at the many seashells in jagged pieces that wash up to shore, and up ahead I saw a beautiful shell, whole and unbroken, half buried under the sand. I felt as if I'd found a bar of gold. I held it in my hand and gazed at all the details of God's love so carefully etched into every perfect line and curve of this tiny creation. I put the shell in my pocket and kept walking, and a bit farther down the shoreline I found another shell, almost identical to the one I'd found before, but this one was broken. The beautiful lines were wrought with jagged edges and the missing pieces of this shell were floating somewhere in the vast sea.

It made me think. Like the first shell, we all start out in this world beautiful and whole. Some of us get by in life without being broken or crushed by the waves or the predators. Others of us aren't so fortunate.

I thought Hollis and I were kind of like that broken shell, once perfect but now broken. Maybe Hollis was simply reaching out for something to make him whole again. Then I wondered, isn't that what we are all doing?

Hollis, as far as anyone ever knew, never had a girlfriend. Or a boyfriend for that matter. He never left Cumberland Gap. Never took a trip to the beach or to Washington, DC.

He chose to live as a sort of nomad between Tennessee and Kentucky, there where the two states abide close together. Through the kindness of a man in Harrogate, a room was made available to Hollis in Bill Parson's large old house. Folks saw Hollis for the very special person that he was to the community and sought to offer him shelter, food, and whatever they could to look after him. He was known to talk about God and Jesus, and he seemed to have faith, though I found no one who could pinpoint a trip to the altar or that he was even ever baptized. But he did spend a lot of time at the river. It wouldn't surprise me one bit if Hollis was baptized at some point in the old river in Cumberland Gap, but never spoke about it.

There was a bench Hollis liked to sit on. It was in front of the IGA where my family always did all the grocery shopping when I was young, right across from LMU (Lincoln Memorial University) in Harrogate. He told his good friend Johnny once, "That old diabetes, it'll get you." Hollis had become a diabetic as an adult. In the end, on that spring day in 2011, Hollis sat down on his bench in front of the grocery store. Locals were all used to seeing him there. It was his office, I guess you'd say, where he observed the comings and goings of life.

He felt unwell, and there on that bench, he collapsed and died.

There was a true sadness for the passing of Hollis. He had started off as a sort of sideshow attraction, but in the hearts of those who knew him all those years, he was beloved and cherished. An artist who lived on his own terms and accepted the kindness of others with gratitude.

It made me remember that there are good people in this world who see someone like Hollis and, instead of trying to condemn him or fix him, they simply learn to love him. The sadness of his passing reached to a much deeper place than that of the passing of someone of means or influence. Maybe that was because Hollis touched those who knew him with compassion and moved them to charity; he stood as a reminder to love those who seem unlovable and to give a cup of cold water to those who are thirsty. Hollis, by being the way he was, caused us to remember the call of Christ. To love thy neighbor as thyself.

Love.

Maybe that's what Hollis was really searching for. "There is no fear in love; but perfect love casts out fear" (1 John 4:18 NKJV), we're told. Whatever Hollis was afraid of and whatever we are afraid of or scarred by or broken by could be redeemed. By love. It seems that our fears drive us farther and farther from the healing. Farther and farther from the love of God that can truly heal us.

We are called to be the hands and feet of Christ. To love with our bodies and our words and our actions. For when we reach out and extend a hand of love, the strong arm of fear can no longer hold us.

Maybe Hollis learned to let go of his fear and be content with the love God had placed around him—the people who watched him draw or play the piano or gave him a ride or a place to stay or a warm meal to eat or a bench to sit on. Maybe those people didn't fully understand Hollis and his way of life, but somehow love conquered their fear.

Good-bye, Hollis. You will be missed and remembered forever.

How You Live

WEDDINGS AND FUNERALS have a way of bringing life into sharp focus. I have had two such profound moments, one at a funeral, one at a wedding.

Several years ago our family was attending the funeral of a family friend. It was cold, the weather dreary and freezing with an overcast sky. (I have changed certain details in this story to protect the person's identity.)

At this funeral, there were scores of limousines outside the enormous ballroom that had been rented for the occasion. The deceased was a person of enormous wealth. There were Jumbotrons at the front of the room to present photos from this person's life: vacations in Vail, a beach house in France. There were speeches with mentions of awards won, charities funded, and generous humanitarian work done on this person's behalf. I sang a Celine Dion song at the family's request. There was very little laughter and few tears, but there was, most certainly, a feeling of respect and maybe even a little envy for the enormous amount of work and money made by the deceased.

In all of it, there was never a mention of faith, of a greater purpose. There were few, if any, mentions of tender moments with grandchildren or pictures at baseball games or ballet recitals. Just a clear message. This person worked a lot and made a great deal of money. End of story. Literally.

In the end we left in a somber procession, walking back out beneath the gray sky feeling a sense of despair, a sense of longing for something more.

We returned home and I was overwhelmed with this feeling that I could not shake. I sat in our newly added mudroom, and while my husband assembled Ikea shelves we talked about the funeral. Then I went away and sat alone. This is what writers do: We let it all build up inside until we reach for the pen and paper. I began to write words down, words that became a poem that became lyrics that became a song.[1]

Wake up to the sunlight with your windows open
Don't hold in your anger or leave things unspoken
Wear your red dress, use your good dishes
Make a big mess and make lots of wishes
Have what you want
But want what you have
And don't spend your life looking back

Turn up the music
Turn it up loud
Take a few chances
And let it all out
'Cause you won't regret

Looking back on where you have been
'Cause it's not who you knew
It's not what you did
It's how you live

Some time later we attended a wedding. It was an outdoor wedding on a beautiful farm with a large oak tree whose arms arched over a small mountain stream. The wedding budget was small, the couple was very young, and the parents had been hit hard by the financial crisis. After days and weeks and months looking through magazines for ideas to make a simple wedding beautiful there were Chinese paper lanterns in trees and garden roses in mason jars and the altar was underneath the big oak tree. The bride appeared like a vision in her white dress, looking so beautiful, we could barely breathe.

And then it happened . . . *drop, drop, drop.* Yes.

It started to rain.

And as they stood there before the minister and the Lord, the large oak tree was a canopy over them, but not those of us in the audience. But we sat, mesmerized and soaking wet by this time, our tears mingling with the rain in this beautiful moment and the feeling that the rain was a sign of God's blessing and that not even the most opulent of weddings could have held a candle to the simple beauty of that young couple beneath the oak tree.

There was peace and prayers and thanksgiving. My mom leaned over and said, "Rain is a blessing from God."

169

No one ever wants rain on the day of an outdoor wedding, yet as all of us wedding guests sought shelter in the picnic area when the ceremony ended, our hearts were so full with hope and a feeling of being a part of something pure and beautiful that not a single complaint was voiced. It was such a vivid reminder of the beauty of life and the gift that it is. All of us who had struggled through marriage and loss and failures were taken back to that moment when life was just beginning and the slate was clean with a brand-new page on which to write your life.

I guess a grand funeral in a ballroom or a simple country wedding under an oak tree in the rain can each teach us something about how to live. Not to waste it on things that don't really matter in the end but to drink in every beautiful moment we can.

To make every day count. To appreciate the simple things. To live each day in a way that might bring a smile to the face of God.

---

1   It became "How You Live (Turn Up the Music)," which was released by Point of Grace in 2007 and later won the Dove Award for Country Recorded Song of the Year.

Treasure Box

~~~

I ONCE READ A STORY ABOUT a couple of guys who bought a dilapidated cottage as an investment in Long Island, New York, for about $300,000. The investors hoped to fix it up and turn a profit of perhaps $100,000.

When the two were looking over the cottage in the process of purchasing it, they found artwork piled in the back of the house. The men asked the sellers about their plans for the large pile of paintings, and the sellers confessed that they planned on throwing the artwork away. So the two investors asked if they could buy the pile of paintings. The seller quickly agreed on a price of $2,500 and added it to the purchase price of the cottage.

In the end, the two men found they had acquired more than three thousand abstract paintings and drawings by an Armenian American artist named Arthur Pinajian, who had lived in the old cottage decades before. Time and money were spent having the paintings professionally restored, and when they were appraised, it was discovered that the total value of the artwork, once destined for the trash heap, was thirty million dollars.

This is, of course, one of those stories that make all of us *Antiques Roadshow* lovers drool. But it got me thinking about treasures in my life, things I have overlooked or simply not made time for.

One such thing was a box.

A box that sat in the back of my walk-in closet for close to a year.

It was my father's box.

Over the months, I would glance down at it as I was grabbing a pair of shoes or reorganizing a shelf of shirts and think, *One of these days, I'm gonna go through that box.* But it just sat and sat there 'til one day I knew it was the day.

Honestly, I still questioned whether I was ready to go through the box. Something about going through it made me feel the loss of him all over again, ripping open the wound that had finally healed over. Both my mother and sister had been the keeper of his earthly goods for more than fifteen years, but then they'd handed it over to me—now I was the protector of his papers and words and pictures, stuffed into a cardboard box in the back of my closet.

Shameful really, but I was afraid.

Maybe I was afraid of what I might feel; would I still weep at the sight of his handwriting or the smell of his shirt or the pictures of him as a young man in his Navy uniform, so strong and determined?

But if there is anything I have learned in my life thus far, things that are feared must be faced, so I did.

Sitting on the cold tile floor of my bathroom, still clad in my flannel pajamas, I opened the box.

It had photographs nearly a hundred years old of ancestors that I recalled my father telling stories about. A faded picture of my grandma Tannie, who died when my dad was a teenager, a letter hand-signed from President Bill Clinton in grateful recognition of my father's service to his country for his years in the navy. Then, in a brown envelope that was torn at the edges, I found the pages of my dad's manuscript. The book he had always dreamed of writing, which he'd called *Quincy*.

Early on in my dad's life, writing songs was his great passion. As the years rolled by and his love for books grew, he found himself waking up in the middle of the night with the scenes from a novel running through his mind. *His* novel. With all the kids grown, my dad had found time once again to write.

> *I rolled over in the street and sat up best as I could. I spat a mouth full of blood into the dirt, hoping there were no teeth in it.*

That's how it starts. I found a cover letter he had sent to the editors of several respected publishing houses, along with a few chapters. Signed, *Cova Morgan, December 1997*.

All this time, I'd had this in my closet and I had no idea it was no ordinary box. This was a box of treasures. A treasure sitting in a cardboard box gathering dust and sadness and then—as if I were a pirate cracking open the lid—there inside was the treasure I didn't even know I had been missing.

A part of the treasure was seeing him with a new pair of eyes—as a writer, an artist, not just as the man who tucked me in at night and woke me each morning with a warm washcloth on my forehead. He was a man of dreams and thought and words and so much more than I ever knew.

Yet he managed to bottle up that part of himself and press play on the life he had walked into, and he seemed to do it gladly. But in these pages, I felt a sense of urgency, saw someone who knew the sand in the hourglass was running out and if he ever hoped to write his story and live the life he had longed for in his heart, that time was now.

I knew he was a writer all my life, a songwriter and a guitar player, a man of the arts disguised in a mechanic's blue shirt with a name that was perpetually misspelled by the company that did his shirts. It would be Kova or Kovi or Kove, never Cova. Like those misspelled name tags, there was a part of him I didn't know, and I now desperately wish I could have had the chance to know *that* man. Oh, the conversations we could have had.

I wonder, too, if there was an opportunity, one that I simply didn't take the time to explore in the chaos of my life and my touring schedule. I missed out on the living treasure, and now I must be satisfied with the smell of old paper and faded handwriting and a sense of loss.

When my daughters were small, I would tell them a story about my dad each night, in hopes this would somehow create a memory of him that they would never be able to experience in the usual way. I had no idea that there were new stories to be told, something yet to discover about someone I thought I knew so well.

I think of Jesus and His twelve disciples, walking along the dusty roads of Israel for hours and days and how much talking and eating they did and healing the blind and lame, casting out demons and raising Lazarus from the dead and feeding the thousands . . . and yet they say, "Who can this be, that even the winds and the sea obey Him?" (Matthew 8:27 NKJV).

They just didn't get it. Maybe they could have but they just weren't ready to open up their minds—and more importantly, their hearts—to what was really going on. Doing all of that takes time and patience and denying of yourself. I am really bad at denying myself.

That is what I know to be true down on the cold tile floor. What I would give to have the chance to do it over. But does that ever really work? We can't go back; we must make time for it now.

The treasures are all there, just like that pile of old paintings in the back room of that cottage, waiting for Monday morning's trash pickup. Sometimes we just can't see them for what they truly are.

I wonder about the life of that painter whose artwork was piled up in a dusty corner of an old house. I did a little digging and discovered that Arthur Pinajian was an Armenian

American whose parents were survivors of the Armenian genocide. Arthur made his living as a comic book artist in the golden era of comics; he also served in the United States Army during World War II and received the Bronze Star for valor.

The side of him that few knew about were his paintings of portraits, landscapes, and abstract art—until a couple of guys stumbled on them and cared enough to see what was hiding beneath the surface.

Maybe that's what matters most, really: digging beneath the surface and getting down to what really matters.

What really matters? People we love, people we want to love but don't know how to love, people we need to forgive, people who need us to forgive them.

There are so many ways to find the treasures . . . Only you know what box is lying around in your closet or in your heart.

I used to think that life's treasures were things like success, critical acclaim, and financial security. Now I am beginning to understand that nothing could be further from the truth. Matthew wrote, "For where your treasure is, there your heart will be also" (6:21 NKJV). Where is my treasure? Where is my heart? Where is yours? It is a question work asking.

Here is an answer. The apostle Paul wrote, "But we have this treasure in jars of clay, to show that the surpassing power belongs to God and not to us" (2 Corinthians 4:7 ESV).

In jars of clay and in cardboard boxes.

Let us not miss out on the real treasures of life.

These Are the Good Things

I LIKE OLD THINGS. A more hip and less offensive word for old is *vintage*. It sounds nice, doesn't it?

I like nothing more than to drive out to some small Southern town on a Saturday afternoon and browse through a store packed with old records and radios, postcards and photographs yellowed by time, old pearl clip earrings that formerly hung on the lobes of a woman in her eighties who still wore stockings under her polyester slacks.

I love to get up early on a Saturday morning and go rummaging through garage sales. Last Saturday I pretty much cleaned out a garage sale. A sweet lady had passed; her sister was selling off some of her things. I found some vintage juice glasses and three vintage alarm clocks. Something to remind me of how things used to be. When a small juice glass was considered a full serving of a beverage (pre–Big Gulp) and you didn't have your iPhone attached to the side of your head, but instead rolled over and punched the alarm clock and got up.

I like old things.

Maybe because they remind me of simpler times. Simple things. I like simple things. Correction, I *need* simple things.

Vanilla ice cream cones, bread baking in the oven, a candle lit in the wee hours of the morning, a walk in my neighborhood, a conversation at a kitchen table over a cup of tea with a friend, the scratch of a dog's head, the sound of my daughters laughing outside with friends, my husband napping on the couch. These are the things that make me feel sane, that give me a feeling of rightness in the world.

I once heard a priest say that when he is visiting the home of someone who is grieving a lost loved one, and he finds himself void of the right words to comfort the deep wound of loss, he often says, "How about I make us some coffee?" Something ordinary, everyday, can have an extraordinary impact on our lives over the long haul. As a friend of mine once said, "Folding warm laundry is a good thing."

But some days I find myself having too much trouble wading through the complexity of life to let the simple things, the good things, find a space. It feels like they have been nudged out. Most of us battle life's juggling act of work, kids, church, and all that comes along with it. I personally like things orderly and my list checked off. This is how I balance the very unbalanced (ADD) state of my mind, swirling and trying desperately trying to find a place to land.

Everyone needs something that brings him or her back to a center in life.

Maybe for you it's reading your Bible before the sun and the kids are up. I have a friend who has done that for years.

Maybe it's going for a walk or saying prayers or baking a loaf of bread for a friend in need.

Whatever it is, we can never let the busyness of our lives

rob us of the experiences that fill up our cup, rather than draining it. For me, one of the greatest pleasures in life I have had is visiting with older folks. It fills my cup.

Our culture has changed so much from even fifty years ago. There was a time when it was the norm for an older person to live in the home. That isn't nearly as common today as it once was, so we find ourselves without the elderly—who have lived and struggled and suffered and persevered through life—to bring the perspective that only age can bring to our own.

The venerable honesty of someone whose life is nearing the finish line is a stark reminder of being a good steward of the life we have been given. It reminds us of our mortality. I wrote about one of those experiences with the elderly in my journal one day, when it was still fresh. We will call her Mrs. Brown.

Mrs. Brown is eighty-seven, or eight-and-seven as she tells me. She lives in a nursing home. Her husband and son both died of massive heart attacks. Her only daughter is fifty-three, has never been married, owns a home, and lives alone.

Mrs. Brown's side of her room in the nursing home is decorated with two Civil War–esque antique shadow profiles of her children that hang behind her bed, along with portraits of those same children that look like something out of a Norman Rockwell painting.

She tells me that her daughter faithfully comes to see her once a week on Tuesday during her lunch break. She says that she keeps asking her daughter to help her remember things, but her daughter doesn't seem to be interested. "My daughter is very independent."

Mrs. Brown tells me that her husband did well, that she never wanted for anything. As far as I can make out she was born and raised in Tennessee. She tells me that she has a hard time remembering where she lived or exactly what her husband did for a living but she knows that she worked with him.

It frustrates her.

She tells me that her family always had "help" and that she never did much cooking. "I had a colored lady that worked for me. She was with me 'til she died." I sense her love for this woman, who was no doubt a friend and sister and fellow mother to her children.

Mrs. Brown is extremely neat. Every time I visit her she constantly smoothes the covers of her bed. Over and over again, she smoothes every edge of her antique quilt that lies at the foot of her bed. I wonder if she forgot that she just smoothed it, or if this is simply an act of doing something, contributing something to the beauty of the world that spurs her to this motion over and over again.

I can only imagine the expensive antiques she must have owned by the looks of the rare antique figurines on her side of the room. She loves her pictures. "I wouldn't take anything for them," she tells me.

Mrs. Brown straightens the small figurines on her bedside table. She has bright eyes. She walks every day through the hallway outside her door as far as she can until she needs to take a break. She goes to painting class, to exercise class, to bingo, to the salon where they get their hair styled once a week. She spends much of her day in her wheelchair, moving herself with her feet to and from these activities. There is no one to take her outside when the sun is shining. This is something only friends or family can provide. Her world exists within the walls of this cruise ship–like nursing home.

Mrs. Brown is trying to hold on to life, to herself, to her memories with every fiber of her being.

Some days when she looks up at me from her wheelchair, it is as if she is trying to say, "I am here. I used to have a whole life, a yard, a kitchen that I cooked in, a garden that I planted flowers in. I am still here."

Mrs. Brown reminds me to live *now*. To embrace the precious gift of life and not let the fullness God meant for us to experience to get by me.

James reminds us, "What is your life? You are a mist that appears for a little while and then vanishes" (4:14 NIV).

Fold warm laundry, kiss your kids good night, pray before the sun comes up, make coffee for a grieving friend. These are the good things.

In a Hurry

EVERYONE HAS A DREAM.

As I sit on our front porch in Tennessee, the sun is setting, the crickets are chirping, and my daughter has just invited me to watch an episode of *The Andy Griffith Show*. We live in a small southern town, not quite as idyllic as Mayberry, but close. We love the slow pace of life here. In between traveling and living in two countries, spending the school year in Tennessee and summers and Christmas in Canada, add driving into Nashville to write songs most days of the week and concerts on some weekends. It is nice to return to a small town where City Hall is a log cabin, and the biggest news is whether the football team won or lost. With one traffic light, the small shops along Main Street all close up around five o'clock, save the Dollar General, the Mexican restaurant, and the Maple Street Grill.

We wanted to move away from the hectic pace of living in Nashville and simplify life for our daughters. There are so many great things about Nashville—great food, sophisticated schools, a thriving artistic community—and yet a few years ago, we found ourselves wondering if there was another life for our family to be explored. So on weekends we went searching down back roads for small towns in Tennessee. Through the recommendation of one of my husband's golfing buddies, we crested the hill of this town and saw Main Street coming into view. The grocery store with a church bench out front. A Dairy Dip, an antique store with a flag out front.

It was, as they say, love at first sight. We literally bought a lot the next day. Tony, our builder, poured the foundation for our house on a handshake before any money changed hands and there we were. For better or for worse, we are kind of spontaneous like that. Before you knew it, we were eating watermelon on the porch and pushing the girls on the tire swing out in the front yard. The townspeople took their time sizing us up; some were suspicious of our Volvos and strange recycling ways and the Canadian flag we sometimes hang up blowing in the breeze in front of our house, but after a while they started to call us by name and bring us casseroles when we were sick and look after our kids like a village.

But there was a moment a couple of years ago when I started feeling like we were missing out as a family by being here, so far away from city life. I mean, we did make the decision very quickly. Maybe we made the wrong choice. After all, there weren't any art museums or cool cafés with Wi-Fi and local art hanging on the walls. I wondered if I was robbing my children of a more cultural upbringing. Magnet schools and urban coolness. Maybe people would think we were a bunch of hicks. Maybe we *were* a bunch of hicks! But that same year on a day in early spring, I took a walk down a back road in our town. The buds on the trees were coming out. The birds were chirping and the roar of lawn mowers hummed as everyone fell into spring fever, emerging from hibernation at the end of a long winter.

At least three people stopped to see if I needed a ride. Two were folks I knew from church, one a stranger. My eyes began to open to the beauty of where God had placed us— right here in this small town. The treasure that God had brought us to by way of a back road. We somehow ended up here, and perhaps we didn't know why we said yes at first and built a home and started living life here, but that is the amazing thing about God and the journey we are on with Him. He always knew that we were headed here and much more importantly, He knew this was the kind of place our family needed to grow up in.

Every family is different. I love to visit my friends who live an urban life, whose kids take the "bike bus" to school—in which a parent starts at one house on a bike and kids from the neighborhood follow behind on their bikes to the city school they all attend. Or friends of ours who sold everything to live in a hut in a third world country and take baths in the (snake-infested) river with a homemade bar of soap. Each person and each family has to take its journey to grab hold of the dream that is waiting.

Everyone has a dream. I know I said that already, but I needed to say it again. Even if you have done a convincing job of suppressing it for years, there is a stirring inside of you. Whether you choose to listen or not is ultimately your choice, but it is there.

I wonder . . . is a dream the unfolding of experiences that take us places? But what places? How far do you have to travel to touch the hem of your dream? What is the physical location of the realization of a dream? Sitting here on my front porch as the stars begin to emerge in the sky, something dawns on me. The destination begins and ends in a singular place.

Within.

The journey that really matters is the one we take within.

When it is hard to let go of things. To give up control or even to give up on something you thought was the answer even though all the arrows pointed in a different direction. There are some aspirations that we believe to be dreams but are imposters. Maybe a small trip down a dark road. But once we find our way back into the light, there up ahead is a destination that feels like an old friend. God knew better. He was always trying to steer us away from the things that distract us from the dream He has placed within us.

There is a journey to take.

Maybe it isn't about traveling to distant lands, though maybe you will be called to do so. But even in a distant land you can get lost and spend years on the back road before you finally start heading in the direction you were meant to go.

Home.

The journey and the dream, are they really about our transformation? What can we surrender? What can we admit to? What means more to us than following the voice of God speaking to us? Asks us for something we don't think we can give? Or asks us to let go of something we desperately want to hold on to?

I look back on all the painful things. I wonder how my parents survived my brother's death. (I wonder how any parent can survive such a loss.) Things I survived that are between me, the fence post, and God. I think of those close to me who have suffered horrific abuse as children yet their eyes shine with brightness and hope. How is that possible? The darkness that attempted to overtake them has failed. "In him was life, and the life was the light of men. The light shines in the darkness . . ." (John 1:4–5 ESV).

The light.

This is how we survive. This is how we press on.

For where He leads will always be full of wonder and beauty, *even if* in the midst of the beauty is pain and struggle. There is always a sense of the glorious other hovering in the midst.

Savannah has come back to me to see when I will be finished writing so we can watch an episode of *Andy* together. Just as my dad and I once did in his big green recliner at the end of the day. It is a wonderful circle of life.

My friend John Mays had the opportunity to work with

Andy Griffith on a gospel record in Andy's twilight years. When they met, John couldn't resist asking him—of all the episodes, which was his favorite? Andy looked away and replied with a smile across his lips. "That would have to be 'Man in a Hurry.'"

What a perfect choice. It's about a man named Malcom Tucker, an important businessman, whose car breaks down on the outskirts of Mayberry on his way to Charlotte for a pressing business meeting the next morning, Monday morning. Tucker finds Andy outside the church after Sunday morning service. Andy gives him the bad news that Wally won't work on cars on Sunday, then invites the very frustrated Mr. Tucker over for supper. The evolution of this man's life over an apple peel is nothing short of poetry.

Like Mr. Tucker, we can all be tempted by the hurriedness of life. The distractions of our desires. The inability to slow down and enjoy the life that has been given. To find a sense of that word that falls so heavy on my lips . . .

Contentment.

I think my dad somehow waded through his disappointment and struggle and found happiness in simple things. Playing his guitar on the porch with friends. Singing at churches and small town fairs. He found joy and purpose in being a good husband, a father, a friend.

I leave the chirping of the crickets as I head in to watch some *Andy* with Savannah. "Opie the Bird Man" is the selection for tonight. My all-time favorite.

How do we find it for ourselves, this contentment that evades us so easily? Do we make choices to simplify our lives? To dig in deep with those nearest and most precious instead of skimming the surface with all? Will these difficult choices pay off one day? Will we finally come to a place where we no longer need *more*? With eyes to see we have so much already . . . how could we ask for more?

About the Photographs

I PROBABLY FIRST FELL IN LOVE with photography as a middle school student, when I would sit for hours and stare at old pictures in my family's photo album. Back in the days of film, people took great care with their picture-taking because it was so expensive to buy the film and then have it developed. And not everyone had a camera.

Parenthood was what made me begin taking photos myself. Since then, like most of us with a smartphone camera, I have loved seeing beauty or sadness or grandeur or even strangeness that deserves to be documented . . . remembered. I have hopes of taking a class on photography and actually owning a serious camera one day. But for now, the pictures here that are not from my family's old album—except one great photo from Julee Duwee and another from Reba Baskett—were taken either on my iPhone 4, 5, or my new 5s.

Introduction: How Could I Ask for More

I wanted to use the image of my old VW in this photo, but for the life of me and my sister and mom who searched, we couldn't find a decent picture of it. So I searched the Internet and found the make and year model of my old Bug and did a bit of trickery. I took this on a country road near our house.

I was so excited with how the sunlight came along at just the right moment to light up the path ahead.

Ringing Bells
I took a drive back to the church of my backyard in East Tennessee, First Baptist of Harrogate. I arrived when the church was having a yard sale and felt quite conspicuous snapping photographs.

What Is Your Why?
I took a trip to our family cemetery deep in the hills of Kentucky this past spring for the memorial service of my aunt, Willie M. Morgan. Generations of my family are buried there. I saw this statue. It looks so sad and haunting and somewhat out of place in Kentucky. I couldn't resist.

Under a Cloud
My sister Sam (holding Charlie Brown), me, and my brother Mike. The first photo taken after the death of our brother Samuel. Taken (I believe) at the Tazewell Flea Market.

What Is Your Story?
Our family drives to Canada for the summer every year. We always pass wind farms in the Midwest. They're so beautiful, and I am always amazed by how gigantic they are. I thought this looked like a cross against the wide-open sky. I snapped this in a moving car with the window down.

In the Beginning (Part 1)
This was taken in front of my grandma Hazel's house, possibly by my aunt Frieda. I love my mom's hair or wig. Not sure which it was.

Tell Her She's Beautiful
Me and Savannah. I noticed our shadows and snapped this shot. We were at the beach. Because of the mention of shadows in the chapter called Bows and Arrows, I wanted to use this to connect the two chapters.

Lead Me to the Rock
The photo originally had both Olivia and Savannah in it. I asked Bart Dawson, who was responsible for transferring the photos into the book, to make Savannah disappear, since the story is about solitude and loneliness. The photo was taken at Rosemary Beach.

The Lost Art of Listening
I snapped this with a digital camera I believe while we visited Banff, Alberta, Canada. If you have never been, you should go.

Whatever Happened to Hollis? (Part 1)
As much as I tried and searched and called, I could not find one image of Hollis. I asked a friend of mine to help me reenact the way I remember Hollis the first time I saw him.

Making All Things New
This is my mother's wedding dress. It is hanging on flowering vines.

Living Out the Dream
This is the radio my dad gave to my mom as a wedding present. Lying in front of it is my favorite picture of them together. It was so obvious how much they loved each other.

Deep Breaths
This is a picture of Olivia, who loved my friend Cindy. She seems so alive and free in this photo. It made me think of Cindy. The picture was taken on the beach in Alabama.

Blessings in Disguise
I took this picture a couple of summers ago when we went sailing with some friends. I love Savannah's face. It looks so full of questions. She was afraid. The sailing was not calm that night. This photo reminded me of how I felt as I looked out the window of my dad's truck driving to a new life and a new school during my senior year.

New Snow
Canada has some really great town names. I couldn't resist snapping this photo in a moving car (windows up). The first snow we saw that year.

In the Spirit

During our drive to Canada last year, we took some back roads and got a little lost and ended up finding this beautiful church with a red door. It was in British Columbia.

The Fraud on the Shelf

This is Olivia's elf. My friend and neighbor Rodney Kelly risked life and limb to make this elf walk the tightrope. The wind kept blowing and it was nearly impossible but finally it was as if he was looking right at me saying, "There. See? I can do this."

In the Beginning (Part 2)

This was taken the night Dolly Parton and Hoyt Axton awarded me the grand prize at the National Mountain Music Festival. Dolly was so kind and always was every time I saw her after that.

Photographs of Life

My father took this picture of my mom and I am quite certain she didn't know he was taking it. He had a great knack for catching her in a good moment. This is my favorite picture of my mom and personifies her essence.

Rice Pudding

I was so thankful my sister Sam found this photograph of my dad and me. I can still feel his love when I see it. I placed it on the 1920s mandolin my dad received as a child. It now belongs to me.

Motherhood
This is a photograph of Sigmund's mother, Gerda Brouwer, looking lovely and staring at her beautiful baby boy. The picture was taken by Sigmund's dad, Willem, I believe.

Fearless
My friend and fabulous photographer Reba Baskett shot this photo of Olivia during the making of the "Beautiful Bird" video. I remember it was so cold, and Olivia and Savannah were both so brave and never complained. Olivia's intensity is so potent in this photo.

What Oprah Said
My friend Rodney Kelly helped me hang an old-school clothesline in my backyard to get this shot. I love the image of cotton dresses and lace tablecloths hanging on the line. The dress on the line was my mother's. A simple pink housedress. It is also the dress worn by my friend who "became" Hollis for the earlier photo.

Pigtails and Wonder
We kept chickens for years in Canada. In the summer, the girls loved to feed them. A princess dress was the perfect wardrobe choice for Savannah to wear to feed the chickens that day. I miss the days of princess gowns.

Comfort

Savannah with our sweet cat Odie when she was just a kitty. Cats are such comforting creatures to us.

Bows and Arrows

In Alberta, Canada, where we live in the summer, we love to go for walks through the meadow at the end of the day. I happened to have my iPhone with me when I saw the sun in the golden hour shining on the girls and our sweet dog, Hershey.

Whatever Happened to Hollis? (Part 2)

I drove back to East Tennessee not long ago and went in search of this bench, where Hollis sat daily, observing the comings and goings of life. He was sitting here the moment he died.

How You Live

This is a picture of our neighbor's son Adam, who has endless energy. Savannah is in the corner. This is at a place called Discovery Canyon in Red Deer, Alberta, where you can take your tube and ride down a beautiful (partially man-made) stream, with a few rapids to make it exciting. It is one of our favorite spots to visit during the summer.

Treasure Box

My photographer friend captured this vintage Remington typewriter during a photo shoot. It reminds me of my dad hunting and pecking his way through his manuscript. Sigmund has a typewriter similar to this that he wrote his first stories on.

These Are the Good Things

We had a wonderful neighbor (who has moved since), David Gretzinger, a retired engineer from NASA. He was always helping, blowing up the air in Savannah's bike tires and offering to build me a square-foot garden (which he did). Savannah got the idea to build a lemonade stand and asked David to build it "with her." This picture is such a great reminder of the good things in life—like a good neighbor.

Epilogue: In a Hurry

I borrowed my husband's iPhone 6 to take this picture, lying on my back to catch the swing just entering the frame.

About the Author

This family photo (when the girls were younger) was taken the day we picked up this beauty. Sigmund worked all summer for this Dodge Pioneer the year he turned sixteen, but was unable to keep it then because it wouldn't fit in his parents' tiny driveway. A couple decades or so later, he went back to the Bower sisters, who owned the car. They had kept it stored in their barn ever since the day he returned it. They sold it to him once again for exactly what he paid for it the first time. We drive it to church and sometimes to town for dinner. It feels like we have turned back time.

Acknowledgments

THE PROCESS OF WRITING this book makes me think of the saying "it takes a village" . . . There are so many people that make a book really come together the way you hope it will.

I want to thank Ron Smith first for asking me to write this book. Thank you, Byron Williamson. Thank you, Mike Atkins and David Huffman. Thank you, Greg Lucid, for being there through the whole process (and for being amazing).

A very special thank-you to Pamela Clements for asking more of me. For making me dive deeper, bleed more. I am so glad you did. Thank you, Jamie Chavez, for being so wonderful in this process and for waving your magic wand and making things lovely and right. :-)

Thank you, Bart Dawson, for your skill with all things visual and for being so kind in the process. Thank you to my siblings—Mike, Sam, Haze, Tammy, Sherry, and Samuel—for allowing me to tell these stories, as they involve a part of your story too. Thank you to Dorsey Pierce, Johnny Adams, and Geri and John Ravnum for the great conversations about Hollis and for being wonderful friends to him. Thank you, Lois Wilt and Bruce Coleville.

Thank you to Lucas Thompson for going above and beyond. :-) Thank you, Rodney Kelly, for backyard photography
assistance. Clotheslines and an elf walking on a high wire—I
could not have done it without you. Thank you, Julee Duwee,
for the beautiful photography on the front cover and the old
Remington.

Thank you, Taylor Leatherwood, for everything you do
every day.

Sigmund, Olivia, and Savannah—thank you for the best
things in life (and for letting me type in the dark on the front
porch).

Thank you to Kelly Minter for your beautiful way with
(kind) words; you are an absolute doll. Thank you to my precious Pastor Gerald McGinnis for your unwavering passion
to preach the gospel to people of all walks of life. Thank for
your sermons that have carried me through so many struggles
in my life. Thank you, Tom Douglas, for setting the bar high,
for inspiring us and making us remember what matters with
the beautiful way you write about life. David Perozzi—my
favorite New Yorker—I am so thankful for you in this world.
Shelly Breene, Denise Jones, and Leigh Cappillino—I love
you girls. Thank you for what your gifts have meant to my life.
Ellie Holcomb, you are so inspiring. My dear friend Ginny
Owens, thank you for seeing things I cannot. Thank you, Jaci
Velasquez; you are such a beauty and a talent. Mark Nicholas,
what can I say . . . you are my favorite bee-keeping Nebraskan.
Michael W. Smith, Chaz Corzine . . . Such good men. Thank

you for long friendships and kind words. Paige Greene: You are my hero. I love you. Thank you, Sissy Goff and Melissa Trevathan, for being such amazing friends and women and godmothers to my girls.

Thank you, John Mays, for inspiring me and believing in me all those years ago. Thank you to my mom and dad for walking the hard road and not losing the faith.

About the Author

A NATIVE OF EAST TENNESSEE, Nashville singer/songwriter Cindy Morgan has garnered 12 GMA Dove Awards, including the prestigious Songwriter of the Year trophy in 2008, as well as a Grammy Award nomination for "Best Contemporary Christian Music Song" in 2014.

With 21 number-one radio hits to her credit, Morgan has penned songs for a host of notable artists in the pop, gospel, country, and R&B genres, such as India.Arie, Rascal Flatts, Amy Grant, Vince Gill, Glen Campbell, Mandisa, Natalie Grant, Michael W. Smith, Ricky Skaggs, Point of Grace, Brandon Heath, Britt Nicole, and *American Idol* Season 8 winner Kris Allen, among many others.

Morgan's latest solo effort, 2011's critically acclaimed *Hymns & Spirituals: Some Glad Morning*, features Americana/folk-inspired arrangements of historic songs of the faith. She is also the cocreator of the charitable Hymns for Hunger Tour (www.hymnsforhunger.com), having helped raise awareness and resources for local hunger relief organizations in over one hundred tour stops across the country. She has also authored two books, *Barefoot on Barbed Wire* (Harvest House Publishers, 2001) and *Dance Me, Daddy* (HarperCollins, 2009).

Morgan's first singer/songwriter record in seven years, *Bows and Arrows*, will include a new recording of "How Could I Ask for More," with special guest vocalist Andrew Peterson (*Behold the Lamb*). It's set to release fall of 2015.

For information visit: cindymorganmusic.com.

Cindy Morgan

Bows
&
Arrows

Album coming Fall of 2015 with a new recording of
How Could I Ask for More featuring Andrew Peterson

cindymorganmusic.com

f facebook.com/cindymorganmusic

🐦 @cindymorgan

▶ youtube.com/cindymorganmusic

Lucid Artist Management | glucid@atkinsent.com | 615.807.2222

WORTHY®
Inspired

If you enjoyed this book, will you consider sharing
the message with others?

- Mention the book in a Facebook post, Twitter update, Pinterest pin, blog post, or upload a picture through Instagram.
- Recommend this book to those in your small group, book club, workplace, and classes.
- Head over to facebook.com/worthypublishing, "LIKE" the page, and post a comment as to what you enjoyed the most.
- Pick up a copy for someone you know who would be challenged and encouraged by this message.
- Write a book review online.

You can subscribe to Worthy Publishing's
newsletter at worthypublishing.com.

Worthy Publishing Facebook Page   Worthy Publishing Website